GIFTOLOGY

Prv. 14:16

D0889636

GIFT·OLOGY

The Art and Science of Using Gifts to
Cut Through the Noise, Increase Referrals,
and Strengthen Retention

JOHN RUHLIN

Foreword by NY Times Bestseller Shep Hyken

COPYRIGHT © 2016 JOHN RUHLIN

All rights reserved.

GIFTOLOGY

The Art and Science of Using Gifts to Cut
Through the Noise, Increase Referrals,
and Strengthen Retention

ISBN   978-1-61961-433-8   *Print*

978-1-61961-434-5   *Ebook*

LIONCREST
PUBLISHING

*This book is dedicated to my incredibly
supportive wife and partner in life, Lindsay,
and our three spunky and bold daughters,
Reagan, Blakely, and Saylor, who all keep
me honest, grounded, and inspired.*

CONTENTS

PART II

PART III

ACKNOWLEDGMENTS

Any successful entrepreneur knows that there are more people than you can count who have contributed to and inspired any sort of your lasting success. Here is my list, though I am sure I have left some people off from the last fifteen years, but not intentionally. Many thanks to John Ruhlin Sr., Rod Neuenschwander, Ellis Miller, Jim Shertzer, Matthew Kelly, Shep Hyken, Ruby Newell, Brian MacKay, Lukas Naugle, Brad Edson, Paul and Carol Miller, Sue Grabowski, Dr. David King, Scott and Rae Showen, Bret Edson, Ron Jenson, Peter Strople, Rob Robincheck, Tony Carlston, Justin Donald, Katie Heaney, Nick Najjar, Mike Dawid, Bruce Hummel, Dwain Schlabach, Roy and James Schlabach, Ivan Yoder, John Henry Troyer, Bill and Eva Keim, Matt Beachy, Dale Miller, David Hershberger, Luke Yoder, Marty Troyer, Bob Habaeger, Steve Yoder, Cameron Herold, Joey Coleman, David and Levi Troyer, Robert and Owen Coblentz, Abe Hochstetler, Ivan Weaver Construction, Bryan Schrock, Ivan Schrock, Bob Gasser, Peter Kiko, Dick Kiko Jr., Gene and Ame Kiko, Lennie and Bert Milano, Margery Cleary, Bill Cleary, Rusty and Pam Kiko, Todd Pugh, Opal Miller, Russ and Coletta Kiko, Mike Sommers, Dennis Raber, Ed Yoder, Dennis and Terri Brazier, David Altman, Chad Johnson, Atlee Kaufmann, Wayne Wengerd, Levi, Ben & Louise Ruhlin, John Maxwell, Scott Fay, Mark Cole, Paul Martinelli, Rick Lassiter, Adam Kellner, Amanda Verhoff, Bill Dorsey, Shayain Gustavsp, Alex Martins, Bobby Bridges, Katie Miller, Ray Cupid, Johnny Cope, Ryan Robbins, Andy Blackburn, Jon Lauer, Matt Wagner, Carla Williams, Dave Seiler, Don Breckenridge, Dan Curran, John Forti, Beth Anagnos, Anthony Favazza, Chris Mizer, Greg Wiggers, Mark Reitinger, Jan Tarnowski, Todd Harper, Fred Paulenich, John Calcei, Melanie Reti-Ross, John O'Leary, Tom Hill, Gary Baker, Kim Tucci, John Kermicle, Jon Vroman, Jon Berghoff, Hal Elrod, Eli Wengerd, Jayson and Kandis Gaignard, Derek and Melanie Coburn, Ian Altman, Kevin Camper, Brad Conlon, Greg Galik, Aimee Shilling, Heather Rae and Scott Showen, Kathy and Odie Darr, Ben and Becky Ruhlin, Amy Rowell, Greg Lukity, Sean Gebbie, Carl Drew, Brad Weimert, Jeremy Reisig, Kyle Schlabach, John Yoder, Steve and Roy Miller, David Yoder, Chris and Ted Karman, Weldon Miller, Leo and Helen Daughtry, Tom Winters, Jason Lantz, Jacob Herschend, Darrin Patrick, Tom Lyons, John Paladino, David Downey, Melissa Rosato, Jeff Owen, Artie Kempner, Henry Weinacker, Margo Myers, Tanya Starkel, Eric Justice, Glen

Cleary, Eric Stisser, Jeff Morander, Steve Maritz, Dave Estes, Gentry Harrington, Ray Charles, Andrew Rauch, Jeff Rogers, Louis Palau, David Fabricius, Wendell Swartzentruber, Jonas Miller, Paul Weaver, Roy Miller, Ted Gottschalk, Peter Blair, Adam Grant, Peter Voogd. Bryan Kroten, Naysan Gray, Jordan Clarke, Loree Connors, Jodi Berg, Eric Krauss, Kate Benson, Tom Hooper, Steve Brown, Levi Graber, Anthony Kaufmann, Ernie Hershberger, Ted Ryan, and John Miller.

FOREWORD

---

by Shep Hyken

I first met John Ruhlin at the big twentieth-anniversary celebration of Entrepreneurs' Organization out in Las Vegas. There were twelve hundred other entrepreneurs there, so it was a short five-minute conversation. Then years later, he reached out to me when he and his family were moving to St. Louis, Missouri. We met up for coffee and afterward agreed to reconnect sometime soon.

Oftentimes months and even years go by before you hear from someone after grabbing coffee or lunch, but a few days after meeting with John, a package arrived at my office. I didn't recognize the company on the mailing label. I opened the package and found a beautifully wrapped gift box. Inside the box was a pair of custom-engraved pieces of Cutco cutlery, some of the finest kitchen knives in the world. And there was a handwritten card from John, thanking me for "carving out the time to meet." I was quite surprised and very impressed. It was at that moment that I became the newest member of the John Ruhlin Fan Club.

He blew me away. But when my wife, Cindy, saw the handmade pieces of cutlery with both of our names beautifully engraved into the blades—and no sign of a typical corporate Ruhlin Group logo engraved (a big Ruhlin no-no is to engrave logos and deface the gift!)—I knew we were likely to be lifelong friends with him and his wife, Lindsay. He not only took the time to acknowledge the valuable hour of time we had spent together (how much is an hour of most people's time worth?), but he had taken a normal, casual chat over coffee and created what I call a Moment of Magic, one that I will never forget. And most important, to this day I still talk about our meeting and the follow-up gift to friends, to clients, and even on my radio show. I can't help but think about the guy and his company on a weekly and even daily basis when my wife and I are at home in the kitchen, cooking for our family and friends. It was such a simple act of kindness, but the gift of knives has become an "artifact" and a reminder of our relationship.

What is it worth to stay top of mind with our most important clients or friends? Priceless!

And the ripple effect of that gift is not only a deepened friendship. John's generosity that day is one of the many reasons I agreed to write this foreword. John walks the talk when it comes to leveraging the power of gifting and radical generosity with your clients, prospects, employees, and even suppliers. I have seen him send hundreds of gifts per year to his own clients and prospects, and he is always asking me how he can help me strategically show love to my most important people.

The word that he coined to describe what he does is *Giftology*. Because of this idea's impact on me personally, I have used his firm to send some of my most important relationships unique gifts of appreciation, and I have seen the impact and genuine responses they generate. It is rare in our very fast-paced and digital world to see people pay attention to details, such as by sending a handwritten note or a personalized gift; instead, many things are taken for granted. We think it costs too much or that we don't have the time, and so thanking someone gets put on the back burner, never to be followed through on. This is precisely why I think John's company and what he teaches is so important. It is the opposite of what most people do. And because all entrepreneurs and business leaders want to surprise and delight their clients, his business has never been more relevant.

I am grateful to know John and call him a friend. And I'm excited about this book, not because it's a great accomplishment to write a book (although it is), but because you are about to get to know John, and more importantly, to learn the lessons that will help you create stronger and deeper relationships and memorable customer and client experiences.

INTRODUCTION

———

*"Giving is the master key to success
in all applications of human life."*
BRYANT MCGILL

I grew up on a fifty-acre farm outside of Canton, Ohio,
with my four brothers and sister. We were a blue-collar
family—my stepfather treated waste water, and my mother
stayed at home. Our family was lower-middle income,
and I wore a lot of garage-sale specials—which, believe
me, never included the latest trends or an awesome pair
of Air Jordans.

You can imagine how motivated that made me. When
you're a poor farm kid, you're always looking for ways
to make money.

A lot of that inspiration came from watching my grandpa.
He was a turkey farmer who raised nearly ten thousand
birds at a time while also raising thirteen kids. Since sell-

ing turkeys isn't exactly the most profitable business in the world, in the late 1940s he opened Kiko Auctions, the first Absolute Auction & Realty franchise east of the Mississippi.

I remember watching my grandpa and uncles diligently auction off everything under the sun—whether it sold for a dollar or thousands of dollars. Although my mom and stepfather never became involved, my uncles did, and today it remains a family-run business still going strong four generations later. I guess you could say that's what ignited my entrepreneurial spirit.

When it came to making my own dough, I discovered that if I bought candy for a dime at the Ben Franklin, I could resell each piece at school for a quarter. I'd trim trees for five dollars an hour, working for my stepfather—a lot of money for a ten-year-old. I was also an overachiever, getting straight A's all throughout school, with my parents giving me fifty dollars per report card for my efforts. After a while, I had saved up a nice chunk of change—when I was just twelve years old, I was taught by my parents the power of having my money work for me when I loaned money to them and they paid me 10 percent interest.

After graduating from high school, my intention was two-fold: to become a doctor or lawyer and to finish college without accumulating any debt. I enrolled at Malone University, a small Christian school in my hometown, and got to work.

Around this time, a buddy of mine named Steve Wiggers started working for Cutco. You know—the "knife people." He was doing so well that, by the time he was a senior in college, he had become their largest distributor *of all time*. Now, let me take a minute to describe Steve Wiggers. The guy is six foot seven, and very quiet and reserved—basically, a gentle giant. He majored in seminary studies—the antithesis of what you'd envision a slick salesman pursuing. I'm laughing now just thinking about it, because there was not a slick bone in Steve Wiggers's body.

Because I couldn't imagine him being able to sell a glass of water to someone dying of thirst in the Sahara Desert, it blew my mind to hear what a successful salesman he had become. Frankly, I thought to myself, "Uh, yeah—if Steve Wiggers can do this so well, then I would be insane not to at least try!"

Although I had some confidence, I was still scared to death when Cutco interviewed me for an internship. I actually wore glasses to make myself look as professional as possible.

When they hired me, I told everybody, including myself, that I'd give it my all for about four weeks. After my three-day training was complete, I made forty appointments in my first ten days of employment. I made a sale during thirty-one of them and did $12,900 in sales—a new record for our five-state region.

You might be wondering how in the world I managed to do that.

One word: desperation.

I had called *everybody*. In fact, when my mom let me go through her address book, I tore through every single entry from A to Z. I had no shame. If I came across your name and number, you were going to hear from me.

This included Paul Miller, who was the father of the girl I was dating at the time. Paul was a country attorney and was also on the board of directors for Malone University. He was the kind of person who everybody seemed to gravitate toward, a master at fostering relationships. I remember going into his office and seeing a stack of hand-written notes he was sending to people, congratulating them on something or just saying, "Hello."

He also had an amazingly generous spirit, and always

took the time and money to make random gestures that would completely brighten someone's day.

Once, he bought a year's worth of Amish noodles because he happened to get an awesome price on them. That Sunday, all two hundred people at our church received a large supply.

Another time, the university was raffling off a $25,000 Harley Davidson. He bought a third of the tickets at $100 a pop, which was insane, because Paul didn't even ride a motorcycle. When he won, he gave it back so the school could auction it off again to make even more money.

Given what I knew about Paul Miller, I was praying he'd take pity on me and buy a set of knives.

He did. But he also bought three more sets of knives, one for each of his daughters. I remember him saying, "John, what a great product. We'll use these every day for the rest of our lives. These are awesome! My girls, when they get married, will have them for their own families."

I couldn't believe he did that. It instilled in me a huge amount of confidence in the Cutco knives I was selling, and in my capabilities as a salesman. Then I was even more blown away when he said, "John, I would love to help you do really well with this, but I don't know what else I can buy." I was shocked. I mean, come on—this guy had just bought $2,000 worth of knives, and he wanted to know what *else* he could do?

A few days later, I had an idea: since Paul was always giving gifts to clients, I asked what he thought about engraving some pocket knives for them. Most of his clients were men—burly, blue-collar types, and it seemed like the perfect fit. When I told him about it, he leaned back in his chair with a twinkle in his eye and asked, "John, what about the paring knives? Could you engrave those?"

I didn't get it. *Paring knives?* I'm sure I had this look of bewilderment on my face, because I was thinking, "You're going to give a grown man paring knives?"

"All of my clients are married," Paul explained, "and I find that if I take care of the family, everything else seems to take care of itself."

That statement changed my life. I suddenly realized that it wasn't about the knife. The knife was a delivery vehicle for communicating value, making somebody feel special and important—and even more so, showing that *you* valued *his or her* inner circle. I got it: make the family happy, and you make the client happy.

Paul Miller was a genius.

That concept, and his way of living generously, became the foundation of The Ruhlin Group, which I started in 2000 at the age of twenty. It's what helped me become the number-one salesman in all of Cutco's sixty-five-year history, and it's why The Ruhlin Group has become the go-to source for intentional appreciation gifts for the likes of Forbes, Inc., and the Huffington Post.

I have so enjoyed teaching others the crazy strategy of using Cutco knives and other "practical luxury" items as a way to open doors, appreciate the people around them, show their loyalty, and see how that kind of attitude of gratitude can generate an amazing ROI. Secondly, the people behind the brand have been some of my biggest cheerleaders and supporters. Early on in my career, I was fortunate to connect with those who blazed the trail at Cutco to make it what it is today and was mentored by them on a regular basis. I can still remember early conversations and dinners with the owners of Cutco, Jim and Carol Stitt and their son, Jim Jr., as well as Erick Laine, John Whelpley, Brent Driscoll, Al DiLeonardo, Bruce Goodman, John Kane, Cindy Winters, Mark Heister, Mike Bella, Tim McCreadie, Jeff Bry, Steve Pokrzyk, Marty Demitrovich, Mike Maletich, and countless others. They were generous both in their belief in my crazy visions for where the company could go and in providing the resources to help see my ideas come to fruition. Without their generous guidance and support, this book might have never seen the light of day.

At some level, everyone hopes that the good they put out into the world comes back to them. For me personally, it's been my faith in Christ that has taught me that a man reaps what he sows and that the good we do has a ripple effect. The concept of Giftology goes far beyond invoking a warm, fuzzy feeling. There's a life-changing advantage to treating people well and developing an attitude of gratitude—the added bonus comes from seeing it positively impact your business's bottom line.

The fundamentals we'll explore in this book are all rooted in that central point. Throughout, we'll use the terms "Giftology," "radical generosity," and "strategic gifting" interchangeably, recognizing that their subtle differences blend together seamlessly in pursuit of the same end result.

Chapter by chapter, you'll gain an understanding of the science behind Giftology via case studies and statistical research, as well as the power of giving, how to create a manageable budget for gifting, when your gift will have the most impact, the concept of "surprise and delight," the advantage of thoughtful giving over consumable safe bets, common pitfalls to avoid, and a final call to action.

These Giftology principles can be applied to anyone in any relationship—business or personal. Whether you're a seasoned CEO or an unpaid intern fetching coffee, you'll discover just how valuable your investment can be when it's backed by genuine appreciation, care, and consideration for others.

Gifting, and the idea of radical generosity, can progressively impact all aspects of your life in ways you never thought possible. I was blessed to have experienced it myself. Now, it's your turn.

PART I

—

THE POWER
OF GIVING

CHAPTER 1

THE GIFT IS A SYMBOL OF THE RELATIONSHIP

"A gift opens the way and ushers the giver into the presence of the great."
PROVERBS 18:16

I could give you a million examples of how the power of giving has worked over the course of my career, but I'll focus on just one. It involves Brooks Brothers and a guy named Cameron Herold.

Back in 2007, I had just qualified to join the Entrepreneurs Organization (EO), a network of twelve thousand CEOs from around the globe. Soon after, the EO was hosting its twenty-fifth anniversary celebration in Vegas, bringing together all the top people from its chapters all over the world, and I decided to attend.

Now, I'll admit—at this point in my career, I was still pretty green. So although I had just joined this amazing network of fellow CEOs, I didn't know a single person attending the convention. In the back of my mind, I was thinking, "Do I even belong here?"

One day, I happened to be walking by one of the seminars and noticed it was standing room only. People were lined up and down the hall. My curiosity was too strong to resist, so I weaseled my way inside. I was dying to know who was causing all the fuss.

It was Cameron Herold.

Cameron Herold was the former COO of 1-800-Got-Junk? and also the driving force behind the company's spectacular jump in revenue from $2 million to $126 million in just six years—without a dime spent on advertising. His junk-removal business eventually caught the eye of Dr. Phil and Oprah, and it became the darling of countless business magazines and journals.

He was, in short, amazing. Everything that came out of his mouth was like gold.

The minute his seminar ended, a huge crowd rushed to the front of the room to talk to him, including me. Almost an hour went by before it was my turn to introduce myself. I mentioned I was from Cleveland, and it turned out he was scheduled to visit a few months later as a guest speaker to our EO chapter.

I knew this was a golden opportunity, and there was no way on earth I was going to let it pass. I wanted to do something spectacular, something to elevate myself as being more than just another random guy he met at a conference. I wanted Cameron to see me as a peer. I asked if he had any plans the evening before he was scheduled to talk to our group. He laughed and shook his head, making a joke about the dollar being weak. "I'll probably just go shopping at Brooks Brothers, my favorite store," he said.

A lightbulb went off in my head, giving me *the* craziest idea. And I mean *crazy*.

Casually, I mentioned I had season tickets to the Cleveland Cavaliers and invited him to opening night. But all the while I knew the "dinner and a game" invitation was probably one he heard all the time—a nice enough offer, but not exactly something that would make me stand out. I *had* to make an impression with this guy.

Now knowing that Brooks Brothers was his favorite store, I nonchalantly mentioned that I wanted to send him a dress shirt, and asked what size he wore. He looked at me like I was absolutely out of my mind. "Why is this random stranger asking about my shirt size?" He took it in stride and answered the question.

A few months later, I received a text: he was having a hellish day of traveling, his flight to Cleveland had been delayed, and he wasn't sure he'd even make his connection. I could tell he was absolutely exhausted and probably feeling obligated to go to dinner and the basketball game, when all he really wanted was to pass out in his hotel room. Playing it cool, I told him not to worry—if we missed the game, we missed the game.

In the meantime, I jumped into my car and raced to find the nearest Brooks Brothers. En route, I called my business partner to tell him what I had planned, an idea he thought was absolutely insane. Honestly, I was beginning to think he was right. The clock was ticking, Cameron was due to land shortly, and there I was, tearing up to Brooks Brothers to go on a shopping spree for a guy I'd only met once. My heart was pounding in my chest, but I trusted my gut.

I burst through the doors and rushed in. "Here are his sizes," I said. "I want one of everything in your new fall collection, all your jackets, sweaters, shirts, pants, everything." The junior sales associate looked at me like I was nuts and said, "Come on, you're joking, right?"

"No," I replied. "I want one of everything." That turned out to be $7,000 worth of clothing that I charged on my AmEx, causing me to break out in a cold sweat. That was a lot of money.

After loading everything into my car, I headed straight to the Ritz where Cameron was staying. Once there, I explained to the general manager that one of the top business coaches in the world was staying at his hotel, and I asked if he wanted to create an experience that would absolutely wow him. Of course, the general manager agreed.

For the next hour, we merchandised Cameron's room to mimic a Brooks Brothers store so he could pick out whatever he wanted from my $7,000 purchase to keep as a gift.

Two hours later than expected, he finally arrived: drained, worn out, exasperated. I told him to take his time getting ready while I waited in the lobby.

I was nervously nursing a glass of bourbon when he finally reappeared—his face glowing.

Cameron was absolutely blown away by what I had done. "Whatever you want to talk about for as long as you want to talk about it, I'm all ears," he said.

Fast-forward to about eight years later. No matter what kind of client he has, he always asks, "John, do you want to meet them? These are billion-dollar CEOs. Do you want to talk to them? Do you want to send a gift? Tell me what you want." He has done things for me that $10 million in slick advertising and marketing couldn't have. But even more so, Cameron has become a mentor, advocate, ambassador, and friend. I even attended his wedding. His appreciation had nothing to do with the gift itself. What impressed him was everything I had done to create such a unique, memorable experience.

Also, my insane investment of $7,000 cost me absolutely nothing in the end because he generously reimbursed me for every piece of clothing he kept.

When I tell this story, the response is almost always the same: "Well, John, that's a great story, but I don't have $7,000 to spend on clothes for my dream client."

Don't focus on the $7,000. Focus on what you *can* do to make a lasting impression. Maybe you're just starting out, and all you can do is take the time to send your dream client a handwritten note. You'd be amazed at how much a little thing like that helps you stand out from the crowd.

Why?

Gift giving and those "little touches" commemorate not just certain events, but people, places, and things that are important to us. In essence, they become the symbols of the value you place on the relationship.

Go back into our deepest history, and you'll see it—even during biblical times. As social beings, gift giving has remained a near universal for people, regardless of their origin.

And hand in hand with the idea of gifting is reciprocity.

Cornell University's study, "Sweetening the Till: The Use of Candy to Increase Restaurant Tipping" found that customers who were given a small piece of chocolate along with their check tipped more than those who hadn't been given any. It also found that tips would vary depending on not only the amount of candy a customer received, but the manner in which it was offered to them.

Based on these findings, they concluded that it was most likely the desire to reciprocate a kind gesture that in turn inspired a bigger tip.

It's a great example of how reciprocity is based on exchange, often to direct mutual benefit, with many positive outcomes. There have been some historical reasons for strong norms of reciprocity, but a common denominator is the "this for that" expectation. Examples of these streams of research include scholars working on economic signaling theory, sociological perspective on norm establishment, as well as how economic exchange occurs under uncertainty (Blau 1964; Ekeh 1974; Camerer 1988; Granovetter 1985; Lowrey et al 2004). Sometimes the scholars use different terms for the same phenomenon. For example, what economics call a "signal," sociologists may call a "symbol." Social psychologists study a number of factors related directly to and required for exchange—trust, group dynamics, personality traits, and cognitive perception [Schultz et al 2007]. Each of these areas is large unto itself. The fact that so many are interested in the same real-world phenomenon lends credence to the argument that it's an important area in social science research.

Gifting, however, is much more dynamic. The recipient will often wish to participate in giving, but the impulse is very different: it is not only about "this for that."

So how do you make sure that the person on the receiving end of giving is clear on the intent of your gift? One way is to be sure that the gift is also important to his or her inner circle. Studies on human interactions have often noted that "authenticity" is hard to convey. A tactic people tend to use is to demonstrate that some energy or effort went into whatever they are doing. This might even be the origin of "it's the thought that counts"—the idea that one can "signal" or show true caring.

Because when someone does something nice for you, what's your first response? Usually, you want to return the favor.

The same applies in the business world.

"Yeah, I get it," you're probably thinking. "But how does that not come off as being really manipulative and con-trived—like I'm blatantly trying to 'buy your business' by giving you a gift?"

It's a great question that I'll provide a simple answer to: it's pretty easy to sniff out when someone's actions are being fueled by a negative motivation—especially when it comes to gifting. Radical generosity doesn't involve your constantly reminding the recipient of the gift you gave, or holding it over his or her head. It is unconditional—which is a concept that goes hand in hand with my faith. I truly believe in loving unconditionally and in giving unconditionally, too.

Think about the relationships you've had. When you're dating, you tend to surprise the other person with little gifts every now and then, right?

But is that *all* you do?

Of course it isn't. Along the way, you're also taking the time to get to know that person better, showing an interest, taking care of his or her needs. In essence, you're building a relationship piece by piece.

Some of what I'm teaching is reminiscent of how our grandparents would have done things: sending handwritten notes, making extra follow-up phone calls, giving nicer, classy gifts that represent the value of the relationship. It's old-school, but because we're in such a digital age and everything is so fast-paced, transactional, and seemingly all about "me, me, me," those little touches become meaningful again.

The overall goal of Giftology is to make someone feel

special and acknowledged by gifting them with "practical luxuries."

Most of the gifts that we recommend are in the $100 to $1,000 range, so don't think I'm trying to sell you on the merits of sending someone a $25,000 Rolex or a $10,000 Louis Vuitton. A rule of thumb is to think about what you'd pay for a dinner, round of golf, or tickets to a ball game. The only exception to this is in an extraordinary situation: if someone just gave you $10 million worth of business, you certainly don't want to send them a $250 Amazon gift card as a thank-you.

Reciprocity need not come into play only *after* a deal is done. One thing I've learned repeatedly is how important it is to acknowledge people for their time, which is what most executives peg as their most valuable asset.

Let's say I go out to lunch with a CEO. More than likely, his time is worth anywhere from $200 to $1,000 an hour, right? After all, it's his most valuable asset.

Since he has already given me something worth a certain dollar amount, it's my desire to acknowledge his generosity and reciprocate by gifting something appropriately matched. You'd be amazed at the lasting impression that makes on people. Too often we take someone's time and ink nothing of it. It's hard enough to get a thank-you ut of someone these days, let alone an appreciation of the time we set aside for them.

Picture me pounding my fist on a hard surface before you read this next sentence, because that's how strongly I feel about it: *Giftology is rooted in the acknowledgment of someone's time being* the most *precious commodity he or she has to share. We've all been given a ridiculously limited amount of it. So when someone shares it with you, let him or her know unequivocally how honored you were to receive it.*

Bonus Material: Do you want to hear firsthand the Brooks Brothers story as told by Cameron Herold? Go to www. giftologybook.com/bonus.

CHAPTER 2

CREATING A FIRST-CLASS EXPERIENCE

———

"Do all the good you can,
By all the means you can,
In all the ways you can,
In all the places you can,
At all the times you can,
To all the people you can,
As long as you ever can."

JOHN WESLEY

One of my favorite sayings is: "How you do anything is how you do everything."

It's a reminder that relationships are important, that

they're more important than getting the job done or even getting the job done well. It's about employees taking the time to get to know the client and the client's wants and needs, then going above and beyond expectations to satisfy them. In other words: all the little things *do* count.

But it comes down to you. If you're the CEO and, as the leader of the company, you're not modeling that internally by treating your own employees first-class, then how can you expect them to adhere to such high standards with regard to how they treat others?

Recently, my business partner and I realized that, although we treat our employees really well, we're asking them to give Ritz-Carlton treatment to our clients even though we had never taken them to the Ritz-Carlton. So, we arranged for them to spend a night at the Ritz to experience first-hand how much impact those little touches had. In turn, it provided them with tangible examples of how they can deliver that kind of feeling, experience, and finer touches to our clients.

It was important for us to do this for one simple reason: it's very difficult for someone to want to deliver five-star service if they've never experienced it themselves.

Plus, treating our employees well is a top priority, which is why we pay to have their houses cleaned every other week.

I mentioned this in passing during a recent talk I was giving at Google. People were shocked. I explained that, while it costs us $1,500 per employee, the return is priceless. They feel loved, valued, and pampered, having a tangible, "luxury" experience typically reserved for high-level executives.

The spouses of our employees love it, too, and it gives families one less stress to deal with—not to mention that it means one less thing is robbing families of their already precious and limited time together. Again, it's embracing the mentality that my mentor Paul Miller had: happy employees have happy families. Cleaning their houses has been one of the best investments we've ever made, and it also reinforces trust in our company. When we talk the talk, we also walk the walk.

This idea of providing first-class service is something that a lot of companies will give lip service to, but rarely put into action with regard to their own employees, which has always baffled me.

Let's say I have a client with an executive assistant who is responsible for ordering the gifts we recommend for their client base. I always send the assistant the same gift he or she is ordering for others. It seems wrong not to! To me, if I don't, it's teasing someone in the worst way, as if I am saying, "Hey, see this amazing gift? Isn't it awesome? Well, guess what? You're not the one who is going to get it!"

Bonus Material: Do you love ideas for unique employee perks, such as paying to clean your employees' homes? Want other cool ideas on how to appreciate your employees? Go to www.giftologybook.com/bonus.

CHAPTER 3

TOKEN THOUGHTS

———

*"Of the various kinds of intelligence,
generosity is the first."*
JOHN SUROWIECKI

I hate the word "token."

So often, people equate gifting with the giving of a trinket that isn't of much value or importance.

Think about your business: Are the relationships that are most important to your bottom line—whether emotional or financial—merely tokens? Of course not. All of the little touches that go into maintaining those relationships matter, right down to a simple, handwritten note. That note reinforces the notion of appreciation.

When you stay at a nice hotel, you appreciate when the janitor, front-desk clerk, or cleaning lady smiles and says, "Good morning." It makes a world of difference with your overall experience when you're shown that a company believes in the importance of small touches. None of these things should be considered "tokens." They're not merely "little things." They're *every*thing!

These are the small things that people notice and remember as big things. Imagine if you walked into a beautiful restaurant where the food smelled amazing and the décor was jaw-dropping, but the restrooms were absolutely filthy. It would make you wonder, right?

Giftology gives you the power to make people feel over the moon about your relationship with them, no matter who they are.

CHAPTER 4

GIVE AND TAKE

———

*"The wise man does not lay
up his own treasures.
The more he gives to others,
the more he has for his own."*

LAO TZU

The bias against strategic gifting within the business world always amazes me. Time and time again, people associate being a giver with being weak. As if you're somehow going to tip your hand and put yourself at a disadvantage by showing someone you care!

One of my favorite books I've recently read is the *New York Times* best seller *Give and Take: Why Helping Others*

Drives Our Success by Adam Grant, a Wharton professor. In it, he categorizes people in three ways: givers, takers, and matchers. He breaks down the surprising reasons why some people are able to rise to the highest rung on the success ladder while others can't seem to get their feet off the ground.

Grant talks pointedly about the fact that the highest performers tend to be givers—people who give of themselves with no strings attached. He's not saying that you should let people walk all over you, or stretch yourself so thin that you break. There are going to be people out there that my friend Don Dandapani (who also happens to be a monk living in New York City) refers to as "vampire sucks." Vampire sucks are people who suck every ounce of life out of you and never reciprocate any good deed.

Grant's concept of a giver ties in well with Giftology, which is why it resonated so much with me. Being radically generous is not just a warm and fuzzy feeling. It's a way of being that can cause you to be wildly successful—not just figuratively, but with real numbers, real profit, and real success.

The idea of gifting can easily cause some people to stress out. They plan to send out a hundred gifts and then begin to worry that someone might not like the gift, or that it won't bring them any results.

My philosophy is this: in baseball, you're a hall of famer if you can bat three out of ten. As it relates to Giftology, the seeds that fall on fertile soil will more than outweigh the seeds that don't. You don't need every gift to create a return for it to be a successful investment.

People also stress over the potential of a gift gone wrong. I'm not going to lie—it happens.

Once, we were conducting a prospecting campaign on behalf of a client whose targets were worth hundreds of thousands, if not millions, of dollars. With a focus on including the inner circle, we were having each of the executives' spouses' names monogrammed on $400 leather tote bags.

One of the wives' names was misspelled. Then, we discovered that a supplier had gotten confused and sent out typed notes with the gifts instead of handwritten ones. To top it all off, I was on vacation in the Smoky Mountains while all of this was going down. But what could have been a disaster actually ended up having a silver lining. Although one of the tote bags was returned, our client ended up receiving so many handwritten thank-you notes commending them on the thoughtfulness and quality of the gift that it completely overshadowed all of the mistakes.

In the end, it opened the door to conversations that would never have happened otherwise.

Is there a risk involved with doing gifting at a high level? Of course. But are you going to focus on the ten people who might not appreciate your effort or on the ninety who love it and are moved enough to do business with you and refer others to you?

Remember this: the people who will react negatively to your gifting efforts are most likely the same people who would react negatively in any circumstance. You could send them a brand new Lamborghini, and the response would be: "It's the wrong color."

CHAPTER 5

SURPRISE AND DELIGHT

———

"Conquer the angry one by not getting angry; conquer the wicked by goodness; conquer the stingy by generosity, and the liar by speaking the truth."

GAUTAMA BUDDHA

I'm going to get on my soapbox for a minute to talk to you about the concept of "surprise and delight," especially as it pertains to Giftology.

Think about your own business, regardless of what industry you are in. When do you tend to receive a gift from a client, supplier, employer, or colleague? Christmas, right?

Would it shock you to know that I'm all for killing Christmas? It might seem odd, especially given my Christian faith. But here's what I mean: I'm a firm believer that you get the best response from people when you gift them at *unexpected* times.

The Ruhlin Group sends gifts on Valentine's Day, Memorial Day, the Fourth of July, and Labor Day. By doing this, we cut into any sense of entitlement because the gift never becomes an expectation. It's always a surprise, and it always makes an impact.

Here's an example of what I'm talking about. If I tell you that I'm going to bring you a pizza for dinner next Tuesday night, already in your mind you're thinking, "It better not be Papa John's. I hate Papa John's, so it had better be from Domino's. And you know what? I'm on a no-meat diet right now, so it better be all veggies. He should know that I love double cheese, too." Before it's even happened, you've already outlined in your mind a set of expectations, because the pizza is no longer a surprise but an obligation.

It'd be an entirely different story if I showed up at your house unexpectedly with a couple pizzas and a six-pack of beer on a random Tuesday. You'd be overjoyed! You'd welcome me in and say something like, "I did not want to cook tonight. I don't care what's on the pizza. I'm so glad you brought something over! And you know what? I hate Bud Light but let's have a Bud Light."

It's a silly example, but it's true. If you surprise people, it's amazing what comes off as a "ten out of ten" gift versus the attitude of: "Here's what I want and how I want it, and you had better not mess it up."

Take that bottle of really good wine that you were going to give at Christmas time, and send it in the middle of the winter tundra of February instead. I guarantee the response will likely be, "That was the best gift! It was the only thing I got in the mail that wasn't a bill this week!"

I call it "planned randomness." We lay out a plan of action with regard to our gifting, but the employee, the customer, the prospect—they don't know what's coming when. So when it does, they are nothing short of surprised and delighted.

Remember our point about "signaling" and conveying authenticity? Essentially, when you surprise and delight, you're acting in the interests of the other party. With no clear "What's in it for me?" available, it's more likely your actions will be perceived more genuinely.* When things happen unexpectedly, the receiver typically recognizes that this effort is for the relationship itself, no strings attached. Depending on what the receiver is going through and what is needed, things with normally minimal value become immensely valuable when given with thoughtful intention. In fact, many studies have shown that things of relatively low value can trump things of monetarily high value.

The value comes from uncertainty, which has often been examined from a risk perspective, but there are many positive outcomes from uncertainty as well. In this case, the unexpected positive event removes a potential "strategic imperative" assumption (Wilson et al 2005).

Bonus Material: Are you looking for the best times of year and unique holidays to send gifts? Go to www. giftologybook.com/bonus to get our top five holidays and themes to send gifts.

CHAPTER 6

THE UNTAPPED DIFFERENTIATOR

—

"There is a very real relationship, both quantitatively and qualitatively, between what you contribute and what you get out of this world."

OSCAR HAMMERSTEIN II

The concept of "surprise and delight" is one of the key differentiators in the successful execution of corporate gifting, and—to your benefit—is often completely untapped.

Corporate gifting tends to be done very poorly and without much thought. It's as if everyone reads from the same playbook with regard to what to give and when to give it.

My advice to you: get another playbook. This is one of the few areas in which you can still be unique and stand out, especially in the way you build both internal and external relationships.

Don't be the person who sends Godiva chocolates during Thanksgiving and Christmas when everyone is already five pounds overweight, thanks to the other fifty Godiva boxes they've already received. Also, avoid being the person who sends red wine when 20 percent of your customers don't drink wine, 20 percent of them prefer beer, and another 20 percent like bourbon. And don't even get me started on how many things can go wrong with food, given all the dietary restrictions and allergies you have to contend with. Do you really want to be the salesman who sends a ham to his top client who just happens to be a vegan?

The same applies to the tendency to slap a corporate logo onto everything you gift.

How many times have you been at a conference and been given the "gift" of a polo shirt emblazoned with another company's logo on it, so you can be a walking, talking billboard for *their* product or service? They might as well be screaming, "Thank you so much for spending $2,000 to attend our conference. Here's a polo shirt you'll never wear and you'll automatically want to give to Goodwill. We love you!"

They're hoping you'll wear the shirt with their logo and inspire someone to bring it up in conversation—which doesn't make much sense. Most CEOs and high-profile people are never going to wear a branded polo advertising someone *else's* business. It's the tackiest thing in the world.

The Ruhlin Group sends out $250,000 worth of gifts annually, and I don't put my logo on a single one of them. I put *their* logos, *their* names, and their spouses' names, but I never put mine.

You would never go to someone's wedding and give them a crystal vase from Tiffany & Co. engraved with your name on it. So why would you give a corporate gift with your company name on it?

When you make a gift all about you, it's not a gift.

Gifts are meant to be all about the recipient, from the timing to the personalization to the gift itself. When it's all about you and your company, it shows a lack of genuine appreciation for the recipient.

Like many things, a gift is only as effective as the way it

is given. As we've talked about, giving effectiveness is highly dependent on perception. As anyone with sales or extensive human interaction experience will tell you, meaning to do well is not enough. So how a gift will be perceived by someone has a lot to do with how it will be received, and subsequently, how well it works. Social scientists have actually categorized giving situations into two categories: transactional (more "this for that") and relational (which means as it sounds), noting that each has very different connotations for people. A key factor in relational gifting is that it is information intensive and more consistent than transactional gifting; and if done publicly, there is less issue of an "appearance" factor with relational as opposed to transactional giving.

Transactional gifting can be done for many reasons—historical, ceremonial, inertial, competitive—but none of these reasons mean gifts are about the receiver, and the receiver knows it.

CHAPTER 7

IGNITING THE SPARK

———

"For so many centuries, the exchange of gifts has held us together. It has made it possible to bridge the abyss where language struggles."

BARRY LÓPEZ

When done thoughtfully and strategically, gifting has the amazing potential to spark your company's growth.

Our clients will often send photos of themselves on Thanksgiving using the knives we gave them, when their family and friends are all gathered around the table. Inevitably, someone sees the knife engraved with their host's name on it, and suddenly, *our* name becomes a part of the conversation in a way that's casual and noninvasive.

Those conversations would never take place without those gifts, and they don't require your logo to spark an interest in your company.

Strategic, thoughtful gifting provides that opportunity. If you have a great product or service, treat your clients like gold, and give them cool things that they're going to use around their friends, family, and circles of influence, you'll have a recipe for inspiring opportunities where your name, products, and services are brought up naturally.

The gifts we source for our clients are things that initiate those conversations—whether it's an engraved cutlery set or a high-quality, monogrammed leather bag. When someone asks, "Wow, where did you get that?" our company and the gifting services we offer become part of the dialogue. I like to think of it as an innate referral.

It's why our investment strategy is to take 5 percent of profits and reinvest them back into key relationships. If the profitability of a client is $100,000, then we'd consider reinvesting $5,000 back into that relationship, to help ensure that he or she is a $100,000 client the next year.

Our target audience is mostly medium-sized companies

and larger who are already spending a lot of money on things like entertaining, trade shows, marketing, dinners, golf memberships, and tickets to sporting events—almost all of which is fleeting. It's there for one hour or three hours or twenty-four hours, and then it's gone.

When you give someone something that he or she will love daily, that's 365 positive impressions per year for the price of one gift. The return is priceless. In fact, it's not unusual for us to have people commenting on things we sent them a decade ago.

Instead of the recipient thinking, "Wow, thank you so much for the five-dollar koozie that I will never use," you can give a gift that makes them think, "I love this thing. It has been beautifully engraved with my name on it, and I use it every day." It's a thought pattern that inspires people to share your thoughtful intentions with everyone they come in contact with.

It's easy to fall into the trap of wanting a quick hit, embracing the mentality that it really doesn't matter what you give as long as you're giving. Few people take time to evaluate the difference between positive impressions and negative impressions and what that can mean for their company over the long haul.

Put yourself in your recipient's shoes. Would *you* want the cheap koozie? Probably not. You'd rather have one nice thing than ten trinkets that only junk up the house and eventually end up in a bag destined for the thrift store.

CHAPTER 8

PUT YOUR MONEY WHERE IT MATTERS

"On coming to the house, they saw the child with his mother Mary, and they bowed down and worshiped him. Then they opened their treasures and presented him with gifts of gold, frankincense and myrrh."

MATTHEW 2:11

One of the key principles we adhere to at The Ruhlin Group is helping clients redirect their money to generate more effective results.

I use the trade show as a frequent example. Very few companies we work with are able to pinpoint tangible results that come from spending thousands, if not tens of thousands, of dollars on participating in a trade show. This can be difficult—many executives are ingrained with the idea that they must have a presence at one. They mistakenly believe that being one booth in a sea of two hundred and handing out pens and Post-it notes covered with their logo is how to generate interest among their dream client base.

Even when they admit to the benefits never measuring up to the cost, they still express concern over not attending. They worry about being forgotten, and think their absence will give their competitors the edge.

A large part of my job is to show my clients tangible results that can occur when they redirect that money toward appreciating their clients and employees well. Over the long haul, it produces far more referrals and engagement than doing what everybody else does: throwing money at consumable things that just don't measure up. Believe me, I've taken people out for expensive dinners that ended with a $1,500 bill, and outside of being thanked that night, I heard nothing about it ever again.

Think about that for a minute: it can cost $1,500 to take clients out to dinner, and they never mention it again. But when I send someone a thoughtful, uniquely personalized gift that costs me $200, ten years later they still thank me for it.

CHAPTER 9

DON'T GET LOST IN THE SHUFFLE

———

"We make a living by what we get. We make a life by what we give."
WINSTON S. CHURCHILL

Darren Hardy, the publisher of *Success Magazine*, once shared a fascinating factoid with me and twenty-five other CEOs attending a high-performance forum. Back in the 1990s, people were hit on average with three thousand messages a day. When he said that, it was a like a collective gasp went up in room...until he went on to point out that, now, the average person is hit with at least *thirty thousand* messages a day.

He made his point: people can only process so many things at a time, and because we are literally being bombarded every which way, our circuits have become overloaded. We're addicted to our phones, our email, and social media. To get somebody's attention and keep it for more than five seconds is almost impossible.

It happens even when you get actual face time with someone. You might have had a great dinner with a client, but within twenty-four hours, thirty thousand messages have potentially eclipsed yours.

It's one of the keys to Giftology: the tangible gifts your clients hold in their hands become one of the few avenues you have to actively engage them. And through those gifts, you can engage them not just in that moment, but as time goes on. It's one thing to be on the top of someone's mind for a few minutes. It's an entirely different scenario when you can stay on his or her mind indefinitely.

CHAPTER 10

DON'T BREAK
THE BANK

———

*"The manner of giving is worth
more than the gift."*

PIERRE CORNEILLE

One thing I must reiterate is that practicing Giftology does not need to break the bank. In no way, shape, or form do I recommend that you overspend in order to make a lasting impression on someone. When I was a college student who was also building a business, I had to bootstrap all the time so I could save up enough money to buy gifts for current and potential clients. Believe me, I've been there; I remember what it's like to live paycheck to paycheck.

Many people will say, "Well, I have one hundred people who I wanted to take care of, but I don't have any money. What am I supposed to do?"

Narrow your focus: identify the one person or five people you most want to make an impression on, and give them a creative gift that's within your budget.

If even that isn't financially feasible at the moment, then make the simple but effective gesture of a handwritten note to reiterate how much you appreciate them.

I strongly believe that a really thoughtful note handwritten on nice paper is as effective as spending $25 on a trinket or gift card. It's a secret weapon, and one of the most cost-effective ways to make a memorable impression. When budgets are tight, I always advise that it's better to do a classy note than a cheap, mediocre gift.

CHAPTER 11

THE REFERRAL FACTORY

—

"When you know that everything matters—that every move counts as much as any other—you will begin living a life of permanent purpose."

ANDY ANDREWS

When you refer business, there's always risk involved. After all, you're endorsing the quality of work or product that business will provide. You might be worried about a screw-up somewhere along the way. For example, "What if the house cleaner I recommend ends up stealing their Persian rug?"

Think of Giftology as a ringing endorsement of your business ethic. When you prove to someone that you'll go above and beyond, you instill in him or her confidence in you. You've walked the walk and talked the talk, giving them no reason to believe you'd ever act anything short of first-class.

Cultivating that kind of reputation is worth ten times the money you'd spend at a trade show or on marketing. It minimizes risk, and when risk is minimized, people become more comfortable with the idea of sticking out their necks for you.

It's also how Giftology creates a "Referral Factory." People are vouching for you—no gimmick, no catch. They believe in you so strongly that they *want* others to experience it for themselves.

Let's face it, having a client say he or she will refer a friend and then actually doing it are two totally different things.

As Ken Blanchard and Sheldon Bowles say in their book *Raving Fans: A Revolutionary Approach to Customer Service,* one raving fan is worth more than one hundred satisfied customers. The raving fan is going to bring you ten or twenty or thirty leads, whereas a customer who is merely satisfied isn't likely to advocate passionately about your business to anyone he or she comes in contact with.

Do something for someone that gets him or her excited, and in turn, it will increase the odds that that person will be inspired to bring up your name in conversation. If you give someone a custom pair of golf shoes or a monogrammed bag, you're triggering a top-of-mind awareness when he or she is talking to friends or colleagues.

If you're looking for gifts that people use in social settings, the kitchen is your best bet. That's why high-quality cutlery and entertaining tools have worked so well for us. Those types of items grant us access to an inner sanctum, where friends and family all tend to gather. By having a presence there, we naturally become part of the conversation.

Remember: no business can survive without lead generation.

If I've done my job well, then I can be sure that my chances of being referred by others will increase tenfold. Again, it's a matter of cultivating "raving fans," not just satisfied customers, but people who will go out of their way to talk about what you or your products or services have done for them. People do business with others they like, trust, and keep at the top of their mind.

CHAPTER 12

GETTING THEIR ATTENTION

———

"Minds, nevertheless, are not conquered by arms, but by love and generosity."

BARUCH SPINOZA

You don't need to wait until you've scored that key meeting to increase your chances of referral. By using the principles you've learned about Giftology, you can prospect your way there.

Here's what I mean: most of your dream clients maintain a very regimented daily schedule, and it's a huge risk to allot fifteen minutes, thirty minutes, or an hour with someone they don't have a relationship with.

By investing in high-level gifting to prospective clients on the front end, you give them the confidence that you're willing to go out of your way to show your appreciation and gratitude *before* you've even had a chance to meet them.

I'm not talking about sending a stress ball or a koozie to a CEO to get his or her attention. I'm talking about making a first-class impression before you've met face-to-face.

The higher up the food chain you go, the busier people are. Frankly, they've seen and heard it all. They've experienced countless pitches from people trying to earn their business. To score a meeting with them seems next to impossible. I know there are success stories of cold emailing or cold calling, but that's certainly not the norm. Even high-level gifting doesn't have a 100 percent closing rate, but our experience shows that it can significantly increase the likelihood, especially when you're going after the C-suite.

What we've consistently found is that you have to shock and awe someone enough for him to say, "Wow, this person is persistent. She must have something important to say." This is usually done with the strategic gifting of two, three, or even four items, rather than the "one and done."

You have to go out on a limb for people to inspire a return gesture on their part. Hit them repeatedly. Surprise and delight. Blow them out of the water! Make those cold calls and emails from other people disappear into the background like white noise. Even if your dream client's response is not immediate, I can almost guarantee that he or she won't confuse you with someone else. When the timing is right, it's more than likely it will be *your* name that pops into your potential client's head.

CHAPTER 13

CASTING A BIG NET TO CATCH AN EVEN BIGGER FISH

—

"Do not withhold good from those to whom it is due, when it is in your power to do it."

PROVERBS 3:27

A few years ago, I was in Vegas for a business conference that featured top executives from major companies all over the world. I met up with a group of entrepreneurs comprised of former Fortune 500 executives who had an elite group of people they needed to connect with in order to get their businesses off the ground and to the next level. High on their list was the president of Target's electronic division, a very large multibillion-dollar part of Target's business.

For eighteen months, they had tried everything to get a meeting with this guy—and for eighteen months the only response they got was silence.

I knew we had to do something big and bold that would just blow him away, so we did some research and discovered he was a graduate of the University of Minnesota. We then hired a custom furniture company to have the Minnesota Gopher logo and fight song carved into a fifty-inch long, sixty-pound piece of cherry wood.

Within twenty-four hours, his assistant called.

"I don't know who you are, and he's completely booked this week," she began, "but next Tuesday at 3:00, you have thirty minutes to talk about whatever it is that you want to talk about."

They got their meeting. Unfortunately, it didn't lead to the deal they had hoped for, but you can be sure they made a lasting impression, one that kept many doors open.

This is an extreme example of "shock and awe." It's certainly not the only way for Giftology to work. As we've talked about before, what matters most here is the thoughtful intention of the gift. Do some research, tap into an area of interest for that person, and make sure your gift reflects it.

Bonus Material: Want a download with some of my best personal "shock and awe" ideas to open doors with impossible-to-reach CEOs and decision makers? Go to www.giftologybook.com/bonus.

CHAPTER 14

RETENTION AND LOYALTY

"You make all kinds of mistakes, but as long as you are generous and true and also fierce, you cannot hurt the world or even seriously distress her."

WINSTON S. CHURCHILL

Gifting isn't isolated to external business. In fact, it's integral to your *internal* business.

We touched on this earlier. When you look at the reasons why employees stay with a company, it's usually because they feel valued and appreciated for the work they do.

It baffles me to see management so eager to give lip service to the importance of building client relationships, yet they treat their employees as though they were expendable, failing to recognize the cost of losing a good employee.

Most employees clock in an average of two thousand hours a year. That's time away from their families, their spouses, and their hobbies to promote *your* business, *your* product, and *your* service, which all add to *your* bottom line.

Think about that for a minute.

Yes, they are being compensated to put that time and effort in, but why in the world *wouldn't* you want to go above and beyond to show how much you value their blood, sweat, and tears by doing something more than just cutting them a paycheck?

Many companies have this inexplicable perspective that reducing pay, increasing workload, cutting back on perks, and working employees to the bone is the way to run a good business. It's mindboggling. Not only does it take a lot to replace employees who leave—time, energy, and money, to say the least—but how would it feel knowing that they've taken their accounts to the competition, and even worse, intimate knowledge of your business?

There's a ridiculously simple solution to this: treat your employees like gold, as if they were the most precious commodity your business could ever have.

The way not to do that is to acknowledge someone's ten years of service with a pen bearing your company's logo or a catalog of ridiculous things to choose from, such as a cheap toaster or vacuum cleaner.

Don't wait until they announce they're leaving to throw them a party. Throw a party upon hiring them. Show how much you genuinely value their time and talents with gifts of practical luxury while they're on the payroll.

You've got to onboard your employees just as you onboard your clients, actively doing things that encourage retention and loyalty.

I don't have that many employees, but it is a top priority for me to treat each of them, and their families, like gold. In fact, we send a gift to his or her spouse right after we hire a new employee.

This is another one of my soapboxes. You should never treat your employees in a mediocre way. It amazes me that budgets don't allow for $100 to spend on employee appreciation, yet we willingly blow through tens of thousands of dollars on trade shows and logo shirts.

Most people want to have a purpose that is meaningful and acknowledged, and one way we can honor that is by gifting. In turn, the gift becomes the artifact of the relationship.

We're all human beings who want to be treated as individuals, respected and appreciated for the work we do. When you surprise and delight your employees, they get something that is personal, world-class, and congruent with the values you tout as a company. When you embody this kind of mentality, employees will be loyal and work hard to show their appreciation.

Tangible gifts throughout the year are a very subtle way to communicate that your employees are valued. When they feel valued, they respond accordingly in their jobs, their responsibilities, and their accountability.

Apply the same mentality to your suppliers.

One of the companies I respect the most is O.C. Tanner. They specialize in the service-award gifting business. One of their number-one product lines is Rolex. When the Rolex team is in town, they treat them all to a really nice dinner. They do this because they realize that without Rolex and other brands, they wouldn't have a business.

Don't ever let your supplier think you undervalue them. Because when you're in a pinch and need them to run twenty-four hours, seven days a week, for an entire week so you can make a deadline and save face and maybe your entire year, what's the likelihood of that actually happening if you've been treating them as if they were dispensable? The supplier relationship is just as important as any other relationship that you have.

Many CEOs have told me that when they apply the concept of Giftology to their suppliers, it changes the entire relationship. They become friends with these people and get to know their families. In turn, the supplier will sometimes cut them a break, or find a more cost-effective solution that is not necessarily being offered to anyone else. That $20,000 they might be investing in strategic gifting results in savings of hundreds of thousands, if not millions, of dollars.

So ask yourself, when was the last time you showed genuine appreciation to one of your suppliers?

These are real, tangible examples of how gifting is one of *the* best ways to encourage retention and loyalty, not to mention ROI.

Make a plan for how you will show appreciation and gratitude toward people, and view it as a difference maker in your business. Budget for it. Make a plan. Allow it to become an integral part of your overall operation.

Relationships are important. Treat them as though they were a piece of priceless crystal.

PART II

—

THE RELATIONSHIP ROAD MAP

CHAPTER 15

WHO TO GIVE TO?

———

"Give what you have. To someone, it
may be better than you dare to think."

HENRY WADSWORTH LONGFELLOW

Who are your key stakeholders? Take a minute and think seriously about that. Who has helped you get to where you are today? Who will help you get to where you want to be tomorrow?

Then ask yourself: Have I done everything I can to show them how important they are to me in a tangible way? One way you can do this is by keeping a generosity journal to remind yourself of the people you are grateful for. Of them, pick at least one every day that you will personally call or send a thank-you note or gift to. Get into the habit of making a relationship action plan and implementing it, not just giving lip service to an idea that will never see the light of day.

Remember: it's not the thought that counts, but it's the thoughtful thought that counts.

If you have never done anything to show your key stakeholders how appreciative you are, then you've just pinpointed the main reason why your business is or will eventually become stagnant. A good exercise is to practice the act of being intentionally grateful throughout the day. Once you really start thinking about who these key relationships and stakeholders are, you'll be amazed at how long that list becomes: employees, clients, referral partners, industry influencers, media, suppliers, mentors, and your board of directors or advisors.

When it comes to prioritizing them, my advice is to compare their current value with their lifetime value.

I view someone's current value the same way I would look at investing in the stock market: hoping to get an initial return on an initial investment.

Lifetime value, on the other hand, is the actual dollar amount that person could potentially contribute to your dream growth plan. For example, when someone buys from a car dealership, he or she has the potential to become a customer for life. If the experience is positive, chances are good that his or her spouse will also purchase his or her next car there.

If on average that couple spends around $30,000 every six years for a new car, that amount multiplied in increments over the next thirty, forty, or even fifty years is the potential lifetime value they have.

Remember our investment strategy from chapter 7? For my company, if the current net profit of our client is $100,000, then we'd consider reinvesting 5 percent or $5,000 back into that relationship to help ensure he or she will remain a client. It might seem as though $5,000 is a lot, until you start thinking about what would happen if that $100,000 client was gone.

Identify the people you need to achieve your goals and how you are going to treat those relationships once you have them—both internally and externally.

We nail down our business plans and prospectuses, but we tend to overlook identifying the fifty, hundred, or thousand relationships we need for our dream growth plan to become a reality.

Always remain on the lookout for diamonds in the rough—the trailblazer of today could be the industry leader of tomorrow. Don't wait until they've reached the pinnacle of success to show your thoughtful appreciation. Over time, they have the potential to become a contributing factor in your dream growth plan.

In turn, those people can also become advocates for your business.

The reason we don't have a sales team of one hundred people at The Ruhlin Group is because my clients are my best salespeople. They're the ones who open the most doors for me.

One of my favorite examples is an executive for the Cleveland Indians. It was a slow build to sign him as a client. In fact, while I was still courting his business, I sent a few gifts, one of which was a set of eighteen knives after learning that his wife was a big fan of Cutco. Eventually, he did sign with us, and afterward he took the time to send out a personal introduction and advocacy email to twenty MLB teams that he had the deepest relationships with—because he was that passionate about our company. Within five weeks, the Arizona Diamondbacks had become a client of ours.

That's one heck of an advocate!

Bonus Material: Want a free PDF of the "Relationship Action Plan" template we use with our clients? Go to www. giftologybook.com/bonus.

CHAPTER 16

THE IMPORTANCE OF THE INNER CIRCLE

———

"It's easier to take than to give. It's nobler to give than to take. The thrill of taking lasts a day. The thrill of giving lasts a lifetime."

JOAN F. MARQUES

Many people aren't able to see how a client's inner circle is inherently linked to their bottom line.

Think about it. The client gets treated to the best of the best: fancy dinners, front-row seats to special events, and an endless offering of gifts. He or she flies first-class, and everyone knows his or her favorite wine is Opus 1. With everyone competing for that executive's attention, it's easy to forget who's standing behind him or her—namely, significant others, kids, and assistants.

This is the group that tends to be the most underappreciated—and that's where there's an opportunity to make some magic happen.

Again, I have to thank Paul Miller for opening my eyes to the fact that, when you take care of the family, everything else seems to take care of itself. Furthermore, it's a way to stand out and be memorable as you seek to deepen those key relationships.

One of the hardest aspects of an executive's life is time spent away from his or her family. It's just the nature of the beast. When you keep that in mind, it's easy to understand how another dinner or exclusive trip that will take the executive away from his or her family might not be the best way to show your thoughtful appreciation.

A better option is to create moments where a potential client can be a hero to his or her family. Work/life balance is extremely difficult when you're a successful business person. When someone thinks of something classy, thoughtful, and personalized that the entire family can enjoy, everybody wins.

I'll liken it to what W. Chan Kim and Renee Mauborgne

highlight in their book, *Blue Ocean Strategy: How to Create Uncontested Market Space and Make the Competition Irrelevant*. See, most people tend to play in the shark-infested waters of the red ocean along with everyone else, fighting over the same scraps of meat. There's another ocean, however—one in which few people are playing, where profits are higher, life is easier, and there's less competition.

That's the inner circle: your own blue ocean.

For example, David was the senior vice president of an $800 million company. He had thousands of employees and was very well connected. I knew that gifting him with something special was a good idea. However, it dawned on me that doing something nice for his spouse, whom I'd never met before, might be even better.

My goal was to send them an item that was family-oriented, not just something he would enjoy, so I decided on engraving their name on two Cutco knives.

About a year later, I was attending a gala he was hosting. His wife was with him—classy, beautiful, and adorned with absolutely gorgeous jewelry. When David introduced us, he casually mentioned that I was the one who sent them the engraved knives. As soon as he said that, she stopped what she was doing and grabbed my hand excitedly.

She was so thankful and appreciative that it was almost uncomfortable. I was floored that someone as affluent as her was blown away by $200 worth of engraved knives and that months after receiving them it was still a gesture she kept near and dear to her heart.

Assistants can also be amazing advocates and ambassadors.

A few years ago, we were breaking into pro sports and really wanted to work with the Orlando Magic. It just so happened that 7 Star Service founder Ruby Newell-Legner had been using us to source gifts for her own clients—one of which was the Magic's CEO.

A few months later, I got a phone call from his assistant Shayain. She mentioned that the CEO and his wife loved the idea of gifting and wanted to do the same for some of their key relationships in the NBA.

Shayain worked me hard to get the best deal, but she was very pleasant and extremely polished and professional to work with. To show my appreciation, I sent her the same gift I sent to her boss.

Two years later, I was scheduled to speak at an event in Orlando. So, I reached out to Shayain and asked if I could meet her in person and also get some face time with her boss.

She called back and told me to clear my schedule for the next afternoon, saying she had a surprise for me. I was thinking I was going to get an afternoon with the CEO, which would be nothing short of awesome.

The following day I arrived at the arena and was really excited as I met Shayain and her boss, who was beyond kind and very appreciative of the gifts I had sent. But after about five minutes, he had to excuse himself to attend another meeting.

I'm not going to lie—I was so disappointed. But Shayain was standing there with a huge smile on her face. "Follow me," she said.

When we got to the boardroom, I discovered she had lined up all six department heads for me to meet with over the next three hours.

The Orlando Magic had hundreds of vendors calling on them, but I was already one step ahead because of the way Shayain had spoken so highly of our company. It completely changed the dynamic of those conversations in that boardroom.

Six months later, we landed a six-figure deal with one of those division heads—someone I never would have met if Shayain hadn't opened the door on our behalf.

They've continued to be a great client, and I've remained an ongoing advocate for Shayain, even as she's moved on in her career.

CHAPTER 17

MAKE THEM HEROES TO THEIR KIDS

"Generosity without delicacy, like wit without judgment, generally gives as much pain as pleasure."

FANNY BURNEY

Before I tell you the following story, always be aware that you must exercise a fair amount of caution when gifting to someone's kids. My advice is to wait until you've developed a pretty strong relationship with your client before going down this road.

Recently, I was in the process of building a relationship with a prospect in the furniture industry whom I had known for about two years. After we met, I sent him a set of engraved knives and always stayed in contact. Although he wasn't yet a client, it got to a point where I felt comfortable enough to get a little more personal with our gifting.

He was on the road fairly often, traveling two or three days a week, week after week, which was hard—especially since he had three young kids. I'm sure, like anybody, he experienced a certain amount of guilt for being away from home so often, which isn't unusual—every executive feels that tug.

When I found out he was taking his family to Disney World, I reached out to a well-connected friend from Orlando named George McNeilly, and he had a crazy basket of goodies put together—about $300 worth of flowers, candies, and chocolates, along with the coup de grace—a note from Mickey Mouse.

The kids absolutely flipped out, they were so excited. He sent me pictures and a text saying that his kids were over the moon, and in turn, so was he.

It's something they talked about for weeks after—and still do, to this day. It's a memory the entire family will continue to cherish for a long time. In turn, it's an amazing cost per impression for our company.

PART III

—

GIFTING GUIDELINES

CHAPTER 18

ARE YOU GIVING A PROMOTION OR A GIFT?

—

"Generosity consists not of the sum given, but the manner in which it is bestowed."

GHANDI

Is it a promotion or a gift? This goes back to the idea of making sure something is personalized and not just branded. If it's something all about them, it's a gift. If it's brand-focused and all about you (i.e., your colors, your logo, what you love), it's a promotion.

When I give clients a catalog to source gifts from, often

they will point to an item and say, "I like this." My response is always, "Okay. But is the gift for you or is it for your client?" At which point they usually respond with a sheepish grin. We've all been guilty of doing the exact same thing.

There's great appeal to a personalized gift. It's the "name-letter effect"—a person's tendency to favor the letters of his or her own name over the rest of the alphabet. That's because our brains processed our names as one of the sweetest words it will ever hear or see.

It happens all the time, whether someone is making $20,000 a year or $2 billion. They'll personalize coffee cups, license plates, clothes. Even when we're not plastering our name onto something, we're actively looking for an item that is uniquely *us*. We even turn our iPhone cases into statements about who we are.

Yet we tend to forget all of this when it comes to gifting in the business world. Think about it this way: If your wife wants a new Louis Vuitton handbag, would you personalize it by monogramming *your* initials on it, or *hers*?

One of the greatest gifting sins is not tailoring the gift to reflect the receiver. When you don't, you end up with something that's devoid of feeling, making that person feel like just one *of* a million, not one *in* a million.

Remember to keep the details in mind: the packaging, the engraving, the occasion. If someone travels a lot, find him or her a high-quality travel bag and have it monogrammed with his or her initials as a gift celebrating the anniversary of your partnership.

Personalization is what turns an ordinary gift into an extraordinary one.

CHAPTER 19

IS YOUR GIFT BEST IN CLASS?

"We make a living by what we get, but we make a life by what we give."
WINSTON CHURCHILL

If you're claiming that your product or service is best in class, then your gifts should be, too.

Giftology is all about consistency: talking the talk and walking the walk. Don't tell everyone that you're first-class, and then send out plastic-keychain beer openers with your logo on them.

Your gifts should always align with your core values.

Because in the end, giving something that reflects the personality of your client in a thoughtful, meaningful way will ultimately reflect on your own character—from both a personal and a business perspective.

Prior to working with The Ruhlin Group, a client had taken his own stab at radical generosity by gifting a watch to his key stakeholders. Because the watch was something everyone would see, he believed it could ignite a conversation in which his name would be brought up. On the surface, it had seemed like a great idea.

The problem was that he had $100 to spend for each gift, and so he decided to go with a Fossil watch. Nothing against Fossil, but his target list was comprised of very successful business owners—the kind that most likely already owned a Rolex.

Had we been working on their behalf, we would have instead taken their budget into consideration and recommended that they focus on items that were best in class. It would have been better for them to buy a beautifully handcrafted $50 coffee mug instead of a $100 Fossil watch that ended up being tucked away in a drawer or given to someone else. In the end, they would have spent less money and made more impact.

Always ask yourself: "What can we buy that's best in class that is within our budget?" Be honest about what you can afford. If you can spend more, don't cut corners. Remember: it's about figuring out the *most* you can do, not the least.

This concept of doing the most versus the least is a powerful illustration of an important idea. In many situations, our minds are looking at something from a specific point of view. Very few things are as objective as they might seem at first, so how they are framed is important.

Social scientists of all types have looked extensively at framing. How something is depicted, which in turn sets a minimum expectation level, can affect a number of situations. An old sales tactic involves taking something that might be viewed as a cost and "framing" it as an investment.

Since framing is a cognitive idea that is learned, people have much more control over how things are categorized than you might think. For our purposes, this means that how the gift is "framed" matters a lot. One way to positively frame your action is by demonstrating consistency. When we have consistency, there is an expectation of behavior that connotes many positive benefits. Should something be misunderstood or done incorrectly, fewer problems exist between the parties when they know what to expect. At the core of the highly popular "power of positive thinking" idea is to reframe or reexamine situations within a different set of expectations so as to improve one's feelings about the outcome. Once again, perception plays an important role.

Researchers in organizational dynamics have noted that routines—that is, patterns of behavior—can exist beyond the individual level. In fact, routines are often a key organizational differentiator between those that are successful and those that are not. These patterns of behavior can be taught by individuals in the organization so that others can learn the steps needed to help frame how they interact with clients, colleagues, or anybody, really. The ability to scale or generalize these "routines" is really just systematically living the authenticity needed for Giftology to work. In order for that gift to be perceived as world-class, everyone who represents you needs to be operating at a similar level of performance.

CHAPTER 20

IS IT TRULY UNIQUE?

—

"A generous person will prosper; whoever refreshes others will be refreshed."
PROVERBS 11:25

There's no arguing that handmade is always best. Ideally, you should gift something that you can't find in stores. Imagine sourcing an item from Target and having your client and his family walk in and see the gift you sent them on clearance for 70 percent off.

That's not to say that sourcing from a known vendor is the worst thing you could possibly do. Just be thoughtful about what you're purchasing.

Locally sourced items are a great way to go. Check around and see what kind of vendors you have right in your own backyard. You'd be amazed at the number of uniquely merchandised retail shops that could truly benefit from a partnership with you. People have become more interested in supporting local businesses and knowing where a product originated from, which is why The Ruhlin Group actively looks for items crafted in the United States.

As a general rule, if something is available in a big-box store like Walmart or Macy's, we're not sourcing that item as a potential gift. The higher up the food chain you go, the more this matters. Remember: exclusive doesn't always mean expensive. I use the term "practical luxury" because, sure, you can go the Louis Vuitton route, but it's usually not necessary. It's simply a matter of making your gift unique, memorable, and personal.

One mistake I see businesses making time and time again is the desire to gift people with Apple products, simply because they know how wildly popular the brand is with consumers.

Here's the problem—very few people *don't* have an iPod, iPhone, or iPad these days. When they receive a duplicate, it's often given away.

My advice is to stay away from these and similar old standbys: nuts, chocolate, food or fruit baskets, gift cards from Amazon or Starbucks, a polo shirt or pullover, and cheap luggage.

Bonus Material: Want a PDF of the ten worst gifts so as to avoid giving them to key clients? Go to www.giftologybook. com/bonus.

CHAPTER 21

IS IT PRACTICAL?

—

"Leaders should be collaborative, modest, and generous."
BILL BRADLEY

Most Americans are not lacking in the amount of "stuff" they own.

People want something that's of high quality and useful. It's one of the reasons why the cutlery has worked so well for us. Generally speaking, most people have never been gifted with an engraved, high-end knife, even though eating is universal and cooking has become cool.

Remember my friend Don Dandapani, the monk I mentioned in Chapter 4? He occupies a studio apartment in New York City and maintains a very minimal lifestyle, purging the junk he accumulates every year. The knife we gifted him is something he chooses to keep because of how often it is used.

People appreciate gifts that don't add to the clutter, that they can use and enjoy frequently—even more so when it's an item that they wouldn't ordinarily buy for themselves.

That's how you surprise and delight.

CHAPTER 22

WILL IT BE VISIBLE?

———

*"Whoever sows generously will
also reap generously."*

2 CORINTHIANS 9:6

Your gift should be a conversation starter, something that by its very nature will keep you on top of someone's mind. Your best gift for ROI is something that's used daily versus only a dozen times a year.

Even if that heightened visibility doesn't turn into an instant referral, it has the potential to spark a conversation about what you do or who you are. You'd be amazed at the number of doors it can open—some of which may prove to be immensely lucrative. Because the cutlery we give is used in the kitchen on an almost daily basis, it's as if we were a permanent guest at every meal. That has proven to be just as valuable as if we were there ourselves.

We've had clients take pictures of themselves using their nine-inch chef knife with a big grin on their face at Christmas, Hanukkah, Easter, and the Fourth of July.

We've also had success in gifting items for use on the golf course. Most golfers have a little accessories pouch to hold their personal items—but most are made of canvas. We gift one made of high-quality leather. The reason is that $75 for a leather accessories pouch has a greater impact than a $200 club that the golfer probably already has in his possession.

Pick a visible item that will be used frequently, and find the most exquisite one of its kind that you can afford to gift.

CHAPTER 23

IS IT LASTING?

—

"The heart that gives, gathers."
TAO TE CHING

It's understandable why companies tend to gift consumable products around the holidays: Godiva chocolates, HoneyBaked hams, or Harry & David fruit baskets. It's quick, easy, and people have come to expect it—which is exactly what you don't want.

Instead of gifting your clients with something that will register as a blip on the radar, choose an item that will serve as the artifact of your relationship, something that becomes woven into the very fabric of their lives.

A friend of mine, Joey Coleman, is one of the top-rated motivational speakers in the world. He's also a former attorney. Years ago, he had a client who left a $5 million estate to his three grown children. Over the course of the next five years, those kids managed to lose the entire $5 million because they were fighting over one thing.

Joey likes to pause at this point in the story so people can guess what they were fighting over. Priceless work of art? Gorgeous beachfront home on a tropical island? Fancy cars?

Nope.

Those kids blew through $5 million fighting over a $20 harmonica that their father had played every night after dinner for the past forty years.

It wasn't the harmonica they cared about per se—it was what that harmonica represented. It was a deeply treasured artifact that triggered the memory of hundreds of dinners spent with their father over the years.

I like to keep that in mind when it comes to strategic gifting. If you choose wisely, you can often tap into someone's deep, emotional memory bank. That's what makes the difference between a lasting impression and a flash in the pan.

CHAPTER 24

IS IT UNIVERSAL?

"For it is in giving that we receive."
FRANCIS OF ASSISI

Making a gift personalized doesn't mean it can't be universally given.

When you're gifting for multiple people, it's unlikely you'll be able to handpick one unique item for each individual recipient.

You can find thoughtful, unique gifts that can be used universally, aren't gender-specific, and are generally safe bets. It's why we rely so heavily on practical, everyday luxuries—leather laptop bags, toiletry bags, golfer's accessories pouches, and portfolios; over-the-ear headphones; metal canteens that can keep liquids hot or cold for twenty-four hours; or custom-fitted clothing.

Such items are also relatively safe bets. The last thing we'd want to do is source some really wonderful wine for an entire client base only to discover that a handful of recipients are recovering alcoholics. However, if you know your client is a wine aficionado, it'd be more than appropriate to send him or her a Code38 wine key. If the client love scotch, send him or her Refresh highball glasses made from recycled wine bottles.

Again, it's not the thought that counts. It's the thoughtful thought that counts.

Simply be conscientious of the types of gifts you are sending out. As you develop your relationships, you'll find inspiration from their likes and dislikes. Until that happens, just be careful of the land mines: gluten allergies, dietary restrictions, addiction issues. There are a million ways you can offend people with gifts.

When done correctly, though, there are also a million ways you can surprise and delight.

When you put Giftology into practice the right way, the

impact is a hundred times more valuable than the risk. Don't let the land mines scare you—just take a more thoughtful approach.

CHAPTER 25

DO YOU HAVE A LONG-TERM PLAN?

———

"Really big people are, above everything else, courteous, considerate and generous—not just to some people in some circumstances— but to everyone all the time."

THOMAS J. WATSON

Many people get overwhelmed with the whole concept of Giftology, so they end up doing nothing at all.

Giftology is not about stressing yourself out or feeling as though there's no way any of this can be accomplished unless you have a budget of $1 million. There are practical and doable options that will allow you to make a long and lasting impression on people.

It always helps to plan ahead, just as you would for any other strategic business practice. Identify whether gifting is something you can handle internally or if you will need to outsource. Establish a budget. Then, identify your key stakeholders and begin sourcing some universal practical luxuries to gift them with.

This systematic approach embeds Giftology as an automatic part of your company's culture rather than as a reactionary, last-minute push for a rush order of Harry & David pears at Christmas.

When you fly by the seat of your pants, there is a hundred times more risk involved: you'll end up wasting time, money, and resources to have very little impact.

At The Ruhlin Group, we implement what I call "planned randomness." Internally, we know exactly what we will be gifting a client with over a twelve-month period. But because the recipient has no idea what's coming next or when, it feels very random to them. It's how we're able to perpetuate the idea of "surprise and delight" in a controlled manner.

Thinking strategically avoids last-minute panic and spending vast amounts of time and energy trying to reinvent the wheel.

Recently, a client of ours ended up paying more for shipping than the gift itself because of poor planning. As a result, he blew half of his budget on FedEx.

Planning ahead avoids such catastrophes.

CHAPTER 26

DOES IT ALLOW FOR CONTINUITY?

———

"Love only grows by sharing. You can only have more for yourself by giving it away to others."
BRIAN TRACY

People worry that if they gift a very nice, high-quality item, everything that follows will pale in comparison.

You can easily combat that concern by focusing on items that aren't simply a "one and done." In other words, think of each gift as one in a cohesive series.

We do that with leather goods. We might send a bag, then

a portfolio, and then a journal, so there's some conti-nuity to what we're giving—it's not just a smattering of random gifts.

This is especially important for your ongoing relation-ships, since it's unlikely you'll be sending only one gift of appreciation a year. When we plan to send out something in February, we think about what the add-on will be for May. I might purchase a $3,000 cutlery set to send in increments: first the carving knives, then the chef's knives, and so on. By breaking it up, you also avoid creating an uncomfortable scenario for your recipient, who might begin to wonder what you "want" in return for such an expensive gift.

Think congruently: figure out whether it's cutlery or leather goods or something else that can be broken apart into bite-sized pieces, and then plan ahead for one year or two years. We've worked with companies who know exactly what they are going to be gifting to their clients over the next ten years.

CHAPTER 27

WHAT WOULD THEY REALLY WANT?

"It is better to give than to receive."

ACTS 20:35

When my wife, Lindsay, and I began dating, my career was going through a huge transition.

Upon selling half of my business, I found out that my assistant had been stealing from me. Since she was also my CPA, it wasn't long before I received notice of an IRS audit. Around that same time, my partner and I were struggling with some horrifically bad investments I had made before he came on board. With everything going on, I quickly went from making really good money to living on $1,000 a month, barely keeping my head above water.

To make matters even worse, my immediate family experienced a heartbreaking, personal tragedy.

Everything seemed to be crumbling. Lindsay had just moved from St. Louis to Ohio so we could be together, but I was so busy I was barely around.

It was a very, very low point in my life—not exactly the greatest time to start a relationship.

After some time, things began to turn around, although slowly. My financial outlook had brightened enough to where it seemed like a good time to pop the question.

A job opportunity had taken Lindsay back to St. Louis, and with Valentine's Day approaching, we agreed she would fly to Ohio so we could spend the weekend together.

Lindsay had become a bright light in my life. She was invaluable to me, having stood by my side while I went through the valley of all valleys—both professionally and personally. I desperately wanted her to experience a proposal that would blow her mind—better than anything I'd ever done for a client.

My plan would be set in motion with my brother Travis and me flying to St. Louis a few hours ahead of her scheduled departure. Once there, we'd go into the bathroom and use special-effects makeup to transform me into an eighty-five-year old man: false teeth, bifocals, and enough bulk to make me look 150 pounds heavier.

Since our favorite movie was *The Notebook*—yes, I'm a sap—I had created one of our own, writing out fifty pages of memories in a journal, details she never would have expected me to remember. I had the back carved out with a compartment to hold the ring box and recorded what I had written onto an iPod Mini.

While Lindsay was waiting to board, my brother would deliver the package to her along with instructions to read and listen to the first half while on the ground, and wait until she had reached altitude to finish the remainder.

I had already arranged with Continental to purchase the seat next to hers. The idea was that by the time she got toward the end of our notebook—namely, the part about growing old together—the "old guy" sitting next to her would drop down on one knee at 30,000 feet.

That was my epic plan.

Here's what actually happened.

On the day of her departure, my brother and I landed in St. Louis on time, and my transformation went off without a hitch. While I was sitting a few rows away at the gate, Travis delivered her package.

Naturally, this struck her as odd. Why would my brother be in St. Louis to give her a package? Cautiously excited, she began following the instructions I had provided. As she read and listened to the notebook, I started toward the ticket counter to preboard.

Before I got there, I passed out cold.

Since I was disguised as an old man, everyone began to panic—assuming I was having a heart attack. Having no idea it was actually me on the floor, Lindsay started questioning why my brother was talking so animatedly to airport security. That's when her mind began to race, trying to piece together everything that was happening.

When my wig fell off as they rolled me over, she realized who it was and rushed to my side.

By this time, it was mass chaos. Exacerbating matters was the fact that this was a post–September 11 world, where cute disguises don't go over so well with airport security or law enforcement. Still thinking it was a heart attack, a defibrillator was used to shock me as Lindsay looked on in complete horror.

She still had no idea why I was there or why I was disguised as an old man. Because it had turned into such a dire situation, Travis had decided not to tell her about the engagement. At this point, no one was sure I was even going to live.

With paramedics desperately trying to revive me, neither she nor Travis was permitted to ride in the ambulance. As anyone could guess, Lindsay was in complete shock, feeling absolutely helpless. Riding to the hospital in a police car, all she could do was pray, leaning on her strong Christian faith during one of the worst moments of her life.

As soon as they arrived at the hospital, the policeman asked for proof of my plan. Travis gave him the notebook I had created, and that's how Lindsay found out about the proposal.

Because I had also enlisted her family to participate in my epic plan, they had driven to Ohio, waiting with close friends to surprise her when we arrived at our favorite restaurant. So not only did she have no idea if I was going to live, but her support system was hundreds of miles away.

While her family drove back to St. Louis throughout the night, Lindsay stayed at my side to ensure I wouldn't pull the breathing tube out of my mouth, since I was in an induced coma. The doctors had no idea what had happened, whether I had brain damage or other permanent repercussions from being unconscious.

Following a grueling twenty-four hours, I finally began to stabilize. After running a series of tests, they determined I had suffered a seizure due to extremely low blood sugar. I had been on a very strict eating regimen, and with virtually no carbs in my system, the stress of planning the engagement had been too much. When the defibrillator shocked me, it shut all of my systems down.

Although I was conscious, I was still so high on painkillers that when Lindsay explained what had happened, I began to laugh.

It's always been in my nature to diffuse any situation that way, and I like to joke around a lot—which is not a very good idea when you've just absolutely traumatized the person you love most in the world. I didn't understand why she didn't find it amusing. I was okay; I had lived. What a great story!

But it wasn't a great story for Lindsay. She wasn't big on surprises to begin with, and this wasn't exactly turning out to be the fairy-tale proposal she dreamed of her entire life. In a matter of minutes, she went from happily getting on a plane to visit her boyfriend to being escorted to a hospital not knowing whether he was going to live.

We got engaged a few days later, but the entire experience had left her feeling raw and vulnerable. It actually clouded the first few years of our marriage, and for the longest time, I couldn't figure out why. Until it dawned on me: *she* hates surprises. It's *me* who loves them.

Lindsay would have been perfectly happy with an intimate proposal, something sweet and sentimental shared between the two of us. *I* was the one who wanted the amazing, jaw-dropping extravaganza. When people hear the story—especially as I tell it—they think it's hilarious. That's hard for my wife to process. There was nothing funny about it: it was a horrific experience that completely changed our lives.

I was so focused on showing the world how cool and clever and great I was that I completely lost sight of what would have made Lindsay happy.

I'm telling you this story because, in business, we do the

same thing. *We make a gift all about us. It's our event, our colors, our themes, our preferences, our whatever—and it has little to do with the recipient.*

Be thoughtful about what's motivating you, and be honest with yourself. Giftology isn't about stepping into the spotlight—it's about shining the light on someone else.

CHAPTER 28

HOW OFTEN SHOULD YOU GIVE?

"No one has ever become poor by giving."
ANNE FRANK

My simple but practical advice is to give as frequently as you can afford, keeping in mind that it's best to give on fewer occasions but with more extraordinary gifts.

A good rule of thumb is to send one gift every other month at the most, or even quarterly. Just remember quality over quantity, and keep the gift aligned with your budget. Stay away from gifting programs that are monthly because it will look less than thoughtful. In fact, it will often look cheap and automatic. If you are tempted to go down that path, visualize the movie *National Lampoon's Christmas Vacation* and the part at the end with Clark Griswold, Uncle Eddie, kidnapping the stingy CEO and the Jelly of the Month Club. No good. The goal is to love on them but keep them guessing when the next package is going to arrive.

CHAPTER 29

WHEN WOULD IT HAVE THE MOST IMPACT?

---

*"Many curry favor with a
ruler, and everyone is the friend
of one who gives gifts."*
PROVERBS 19:6

If you do find yourself sitting behind a booth at a trade show, don't waste time and energy putting together what will be one of a thousand junky swag bags.

Send that pair of custom-made, over-the-ear headphones two weeks before the event with a handwritten note from the CEO saying, "We're looking forward to rocking it out with you in Vegas!"

Or, pick out five people you want to create an amazing post-event experience for.

Think about what happens when all those hot prospects return home and have a thousand emails clogging their inbox. They're back to the grind—miles away from that fabulous dinner conversation you had and those amazing ideas you pitched over a few beers.

In cases like this, send those prospects three gifts over the next three weeks. It will keep the momentum and connection alive and keep you top of mind.

Remember what we talked about in chapter 5: timing is everything.

One of the best times you can gift someone is when you *don't* make the deal. Seem counterintuitive? It's not—it keeps the door open, and most importantly, it conveys a tremendous amount of information about the way you conduct business.

That's when referrals and opportunities happen.

Be unexpected, creative, and meaningful with your giving. Avoid Easter, Thanksgiving, and Christmas.

Instead, find another blue ocean to swim in. On Valentine's Day, send a gift that says, "We love working with you!" On St. Patrick's Day, send one that says, "We're lucky to have you as a partner!" There are a million and one national holidays to choose from. For instance, send a pizza along with a high-end pizza stone and slicer on National Pizza Day. It can be so easy if you are willing to open your eyes to the possibilities.

One of my favorite examples of this involves the seed corn distributor AgriGold, which was an early client that we sourced gifts for. They wanted to break into bigger farming operations that held land spans of five thousand, ten thousand, even fifty thousand acres.

AgriGold was competing with Pioneer, an international seed company that had a tremendous amount of loyalty from a customer base that spanned generations: farmers whose great-grandfathers, grandfathers, and fathers all used Pioneer seeds. It was not going to be an easy sell.

We decided to focus our efforts on gifting AgriGold's potential clients with something special *after* planting season—when we knew they'd be worn out and deserving to be refreshed. Since it was summer time, we chose an ice cream theme that would be executed in three stages.

The first thing we did was pick out a heavy, stoneware ice cream bowl to represent the foundation of AgriGold. Then, we had each of their eight sales representatives identify their top twenty prospects and sent a bowl to each of them. This totaled 1,600 farmers.

A week later, the farmers were sent a $40 Copco ice cream scoop—the Cadillac of scoops.

Seven days later, we had Schwan's pack up 1,600 gallons of vanilla ice cream into individual coolers around a "Cream of the Crop" theme. Each included a little note that said, "You've worked hard during planting season. You deserve a break. Enjoy a nice bowl of ice cream, and here's a seven-minute DVD that shares a little about why we might make a great partner for you."

We then sent our sales representatives out to meet their farmers in person, many of whom came armed with caramel and hot fudge toppings.

The response was overwhelmingly positive. Most of the representatives were invited into the home, spending an hour or two with these families. It made a huge impression.

The entire experience was a game changer for me as well, because it paved the way for some very important people to enter into my life.

Jeffrey Gitomer was a major sales guru whom I met during an event that AgriGold was hosting. After hearing him speak, I followed up for eighteen months with eighteen gifts, and he's now a client, a friend, and an advocate for us; and we collaborated together in writing a book.

Jim Shertzer, director of marketing for AgriGold, introduced me to the executives at Scotts, who in turn put me in front of some decision makers at NASCAR. Those meetings are what paved the way for me to enter the pro-sports arena. We've now worked with more than twenty-four teams and properties.

Finally, and most importantly, working with AgriGold introduced me to Lindsay, who was not only my key contact at AgriGold while we were planning the ice cream gifting, but the woman who'd eventually become my wife and mother of our three children.

CHAPTER 30

HOW MUCH TO GIVE?

———

"The generous man will be prosperous. And he who waters, will himself be watered."

PROVERBS 11:25

"How much should I give?" is the number-one question I am asked regarding Giftology.

Gifting should be something you actively budget for. If you do not yet have the budget, rely on the handwritten note, as we've talked about before. But when you *are* able to invest money into gifting strategies, what you choose should be comparable to what it would cost for a nice dinner, great tickets to a ball game, or a round of golf at an upscale club: an amount that typically falls between

$100 to $1,000. Essentially, your gifting budget to retain and maintain clients should always fall between 2 percent and 10 percent of your current net profits.

Again, always ask yourself: "What's the most I could do?"

Since it's not uncommon for us to ask ourselves, "What's the *least* I can do without looking cheap?" reprogramming your mindset might require some effort.

Be honest: How many times have you been invited to a wedding or a high school graduation, and the first thing that comes into your mind is, "Do I really have to spend $250 or can I get away with $150?" Our natural tendency is to cut corners and go with the bare minimum.

Most gifting strategies don't work well, because those implementing them are not willing to go out on a limb. They want the safe bets, done as economically as possible. As a result, they typically reap few benefits.

Remember that slow and steady wins the race. Be patient. Invest in strategic gifting with a long-term view of the future, as you would with a growth stock or asset allocation. Over time, your investment will naturally compound.

I always tell my clients, "If you're not willing to commit

to three years of engaging with us, then I'm not going to guarantee any results." You would never take a potential client out to dinner and demand their business before they've even opened the menu.

Giftology is a slow build, encouraging the relationship to develop over time. It's an ongoing process. Again, it's all about minimizing risk: people need to see that your intentions are genuine, with no strings attached.

Over time you will tip the scales in your favor. Don't get me wrong: there are instances when you will see short-term results—especially when you're prospecting. But even when you invest a significant chunk of money to get someone's attention, that's what you're getting: his or her attention. You're not getting his or her loyalty or business.

Not yet.

It's important not to undervalue what's happening beneath the surface, though: you're creating interest, and in turn, your potential clients are warming up to the idea of doing business with you. One of my mentors and one of the wisest men I know is Tom Hill, coauthor of the book *Chicken Soup for the Entrepreneur's Soul*. He describes this as "putting the odds in your favor."

Because let's face it: there are no guaranteed formulas in life, but there are things you can do to increase the chances of a positive outcome.

I didn't have an unlimited budget when I started out. In fact, I didn't even have money for fancy brochures or an amazing website. But I asked myself the question I envisioned my mentor Paul Miller asking himself: "What's the most I could do?"

Since I couldn't do everything, I narrowed my focus. It was important that I created tangible proof of my careful attention to detail, so I put what money I did have into some awesome business cards—something that would be impossible to forget and that cost a dollar each to create.

Everyone thought I was absolutely crazy. They all were sure I was going to go broke just by passing out business cards. In fact, more than one person said point-blank, "That's the dumbest thing ever."

Although everyone thought I was out of my mind, I was determined to get the cards made, even when it became obvious that not a single manufacturer had ever created such an expensive business card.

The Will Smith movie *Hitch* served as my inspiration. His

character carried around business cards in the shape of a square, crafted from very heavy cardstock, that contained only two pieces of information: his name and number.

That was the card I had envisioned! But I took it a step further and had mine made out of aluminum.

A short while later, I met the CEO of Lowe's at a NASCAR event and was explaining what The Ruhlin Group was, our gifting strategy, and how it tied into relationship building. It was obvious, though, that he was completely glazed over, barely listening.

When I asked him for a card, he politely gave me one.

Then I handed him mine.

He slowly looked down at the card, up at me, down at the card, and up again, before exclaiming, "This is the coolest fricken card [*except, he didn't say fricken*] I've ever seen! What do you do again?"

That little aluminum square completely changed the conversation. Imagine what would happen if you approached gifting in the same light.

We still use those cards to this day, although now they

cost around three dollars each to make. Inevitably, people will say, "That's insane. How could you spend that much money on a business card?"

It's an ironic question because I see companies spending $10 on a brochure that will inevitably end up in the trash can. To me, a three-dollar business card is a tremendously good investment because I know for a fact that the recipient will show it to twenty other people before he or she gets home. Plus, when I follow up with an email and write "Metal business card" in the subject line, people know exactly who I am, when we talked, and what we talked about.

I took the same approach with our letterhead, a piece of steel that costs nine dollars each to make. We use a Sharpie to write on it. People thought we were nuts to do that, too, until they started hearing about the impact it had.

This is another area where cost per impression comes into play. Generally speaking, most companies won't blink twice about spending money to print their logo onto a cheap tchotchke. Why not invest that money in something innovative that will get people talking and create multiple positive impressions?

Business cards, letterhead—we strive to be world-class

in everything we do, right down to the minute details. By taking that kind of approach to two seemingly inconsequential necessities, our response rate has gone up significantly.

It's not necessarily about spending *more* money. It's about being *smarter* about spending money.

So, ask yourself, "What's the *most* I can do?"

Bonus Material: Want to see examples of my crazy but effective eight-dollar letterhead and three-dollar business cards? Go to www.giftologybook.com/bonus, and we will also send you a special discount code if you want to get your own.

CHAPTER 31

MAKE SURE YOU ARE IN GOOD HANDS

———

"To do more for the world than the world does for you—that is success."
HENRY FORD

Before you begin implementing your gifting strategy, determine whether you have the resources to train an in-house team or if you need to outsource.

I recently had a conversation with a business executive who was serious about hiring a full-time Generosity Manager, whose job would be to source products and services to gift to their clients throughout the entire year.

Giftology isn't rocket science—any company can set themselves up to do this on their own as long as they are willing to put together a strategy that embraces thoughtful "planned randomness" to surprise and delight.

If you cannot handle the logistics of gifting on your own, then outsourcing is a great option. Relying on the expertise of a company that specializes in gifting can end up saving you a vast amount of time and money in the long run. If you want to evaluate your plans and talk to an expert on gift giving, go to www.ruhlingroup.com, and fill out a request form to chat.

CONCLUSION

———

*"No act of kindness, no matter
how small, is ever wasted."*

AESOP

This may be the final chapter of the book, but consider it the first in your plan of action.

Go out into the world and put all of this into practice. Don't let it become just another good idea that you never get around to doing. Be proactive. Make it happen!

Giftology is not a liability, a sign of weakness, or just a warm and fuzzy feeling. When done correctly, it's an asset—a way to gain referrals, retention, and ROI. Most importantly, though, radical generosity is a way of life. There's no reason why you should isolate these ideas as a business-only opportunity—make them present in all of your interpersonal relationships as well. GIftology can serve as a reminder of all you have to be thankful for, a way of showing appreciation that goes above and beyond.

Ask yourself when you last made some random gesture of appreciation toward your spouse, kids, family members, or friends. Was it just on an anniversary, birthday, or major holiday? When was the last time you sent someone flowers "just because"?

THIRTY-DAY CHALLENGE

In the *The Five Minute Journal*, authors Alex Ikonn and UJ Ramdas encourage readers to exercise the gratitude muscle daily, focusing on what went well each day and what lessons can be learned from those experiences and exchanges. If you haven't already gotten your hands on a copy of this book, I encourage you to do so. Thought leaders, such as entrepreneur and *New York Times* best-selling author Tim Ferris, have read it, as have I—and let me tell you, it has completely changed my perspective.

Their message ties in perfectly with what we've talked about throughout this book. So here's how I'm going to challenge you.

For the next thirty days, begin each morning by thinking about people—both personally and professionally—who are of the utmost importance to you. Think of those who have helped you get to where you are today, or who have touched your life in immeasurable ways: clients, suppliers, dealers, assistants, employees, mentors, advisors, and so on.

End each day the same way: think about who had an impact on your bottom line. Who went out of his or her way to help you succeed? What's that person's current value? What could his or her lifetime value be?

When you start thinking about what you're grateful for, there's a natural segue into wanting to show your appreciation via a verbal thanks, handwritten note, or maybe even your first crack at strategic gifting.

Believe me, I know that the majority of you aren't going to be able to wake up tomorrow with a $100,000 budget that can be doled out toward gifting your top one hundred people for the next two years. What you can do, however, is take one small step every day toward that goal. By taking those small steps, you'll start rewiring how you think about people and how you treat them. I realize that with life pulling us all in thirty different directions at any given moment, even five minutes of time is a precious commodity. What I'm asking you to do is simple, but not necessarily easy.

Try it, though—take that first step. It is *so* powerful. When you focus on what you're thankful for, you'll find that you do life better.

Bonus Material: Want a special discount code to get *The Five Minute Journal* and a free PDF download cheat sheet to get started right away using the *The Five Minute Journal*? Go to www.giftologybook.com/bonus.

THE TRICKLEDOWN EFFECT OF BEING A GIVER-PRENEUR

Never forget that leadership *always* sets the tone. You can give lip service to the idea of Giftology and being a giver-preneur, but you've got to practice what you preach. When you do, everyone around you will begin reflecting that goodness, which naturally leads to a healthier work environment.

In fact, there is a substantial amount of social science research that investigates whether employee satisfaction is related to positive work performance.

Employee satisfaction is measured in many ways—surveys, interviews, or proxies such as pay. In terms of work performance, there are many important measures—team longevity, turnover, and financial performance of the company.

The preliminary work in this area drew on theories primarily focused on economics and sociology. Efficiency wage theory argues that the employees are "gifted" with a good environment and in turn are "gifting" back extra hard work. The sociological theories argue that employees internalize and identify with the objectives and identity of the organization and can be motivated to work if the environment is supportive. More recently, management research has found that employee welfare is an important factor in organizational welfare.

Regardless, everything starts from the top of the organization. As the leader, if you want employees to treat your customers well, then *you* have to set a tone of generosity.

When you act generously, people take notice. They'll begin to feel appreciated, and in turn, they'll want to pay it forward. It's a natural inclination for us to want givers to succeed because we can appreciate the generosity that was shown to us. In turn, that appreciation inspires those people to lift you up, not tear you down.

1 Thessalonians 5:11 asks that we "encourage one another and build each other up." I like to think that the principles of Giftology echo that sentiment. Regardless of your faith, you can never go wrong by showing thoughtful appreciation toward the people around you.

BIBLIOGRAPHY

———

Agrawal, Neeraj, and Logan Bartlett. (December 15, 2014). "Why Investing in Best Places to Work Is Good for More than Morale," Glassdoor Blog. Available at www.glassdoor.com/blog/investing-places-work-good-morale/.

Akerlof, George A. (1982). "Labor Contracts as Partial Gift Exchange." *Quarterly Journal of Economics* 47: 543–69.

Akerlof, G., and J. Yellen. (1986). *Efficiency Wage Models of the Labor Market*. Cambridge, UK: Cambridge University Press.

Arrow, Kenneth J. (1972). "Gifts and Exchanges." *Philosophy and Public Affairs* 1 :343–62.

Barney, J. B. (1986). "Organizational Culture: Can It Be a Source of Sustained Competitive Advantage?" *Academy of Management Review* 11: 656–65.

Baxter, Leslie A. (August 1987). "Symbols of Relationship Identity in Relationship Cultures." *Journal of Social and Personal Relationships* 4: 261–80.

Becker, B. E., and B. Gerhart. (1996). "The Impact of Human Resource Management on Organizational Performance: Progress and Prospects." *Academy of Management Journal* 39: 779–801.

Bell, D. (1991). "Modes of Exchange: Gift and Commodity." *Journal of Socio- Economics* 20, no. 2: 155–67.

Beltramini, R.F. (2000). "Exploring the Effectiveness of Business Gifts: Replication and Extensions." *Journal of Advertising* 29: 73–76.

Berry, L. L. (2007). "The Best Companies Are Generous Companies." *Business Horizons* 50, no. 4: 263–69.

Blau, Peter (1964). *Exchange and Power in Social Life.* New York: Wiley.

Bolino, M. C., W. H. Turnley, and J. M. Bloodgood. (2002). "Citizenship Behavior and the Creation of Social Capital in Organizations." *Academy of Management Review* 27, no. 4: 505–22.

Bolino, M. C., W. H. Turnley, and B. P. Niehoff. (2004). "The Other Side of the Story: Reexamining Prevailing Assumptions about Organizational Citizenship Behavior." *Human Resource Management Review* 14, no. 2: 229–46.

Booth, J. E., K. W. Park, and T. M. Glomb. (2009). "Employer-Supported Volunteering Benefits: Gift Exchange among Employers, Employees, and Volunteer Organizations." *Human Resource Management* 48, no. 2: 227–49.

Bowen, D. E., and C. Ostroff. 2004. "Understanding HRM-Firm Performance Linkages: The Role of the 'Strength' of the HRM System." *Academy of Management Review* 29: 203–21.

Camerer, Colin. (1988). "Gifts as Economic Signals and Social Symbols." *American Journal of Sociology* 94 (Suppl.): S180–214.

Chamberlain, A. (2015). "Does Company Culture Pay Off? Analyzing Stock Performance of 'Best Places to Work' Companies." Glassdoor. Available at www.glassdoor.com.

Cheal, D. J. (1986). "The Social Dimensions of Gift Behaviour." *Journal of Social and Personal Relationships* 3, no. 4: 423–39.

Cialdini, R. B., M. Schaller, D. Houlihan, K. Arps, J. Fultz. and A. Beaman. (1987). "Empathy-Based Helping: Is It Selflessly or Selfishly Motivated?" *Journal of Personality and Social Psychology* 52, no. 4: 749–58.

Cialdini, R.B. (2001). "Harnessing the Science of Persuasion." *Harvard Business Review* 79, no. 9: 72–81.

Cleveland, M., B. J. Babin, M. Laroche, P. Ward, and J. Bergeron. (2003). "Information Search Patterns for Gift Purchases: A Cross-National Examination of Gender Differences." *Journal of Consumer Behaviour* 3: 20.

Cohen, A. (2007). "Commitment Before and After: An Evaluation and Reconceptualization of Organizational Commitment." *Human Resource Management Review* 7, no. 3: 336–54.

Collins, C. J., and K. D. Clark. (2003). "Strategic Human Resource Practices, Top Management Team Social Networks, and Firm Performance: The Role of Human Resource Practices in Creating Organizational Competitive Advantage." *Academy of Management Journal* 46, no. 6: 740–51.

Combs, J., Y. Liu, A. Hall, and D. Ketchen. (2006). "How Much Do High-Performance Work Practices Matter? A Meta Analysis of Their Effects on Organizational Performance." *Personnel Psychology* 59: 501.

Darr, A. (2003). "Gifting Practices and Interorganizational Relations: Constructing Obligation Networks in the Electronics Sector." *Sociological Forum* 18: 31–51.

Davies, G., Susan Whelan, Anthony Foley, and Margaret Walsh. (2010). "Gifts and Gifting." *International Journal of Management Reviews* 12: 413–34.

Dodlova, M. and M. Yudkevich. (2009). "Gift Exchange in the Workplace." *Human Resource Management Review* 19, no. 1: 23-38.

Dolfsma, W., R. Eijk, and A. Jolink. (2009). "On a Source of Social Capital: Gift Exchange." *Journal of Business Ethics* 89, no. 3: 315-29.

Dosi G., R. Nelson, and S. Winter, eds. (2000). "Introduction: The Nature and Dynamics of Organizational Capabilities." In *The Nature and Dynamics of Organizational Capabilities*. New York: Oxford University Press. 1-24.

Druckman, J. (2001). "Using Credible Advice to Overcome Framing Effects." *Journal of Law, Economics, and Organization* 17, no. 1: 62-82.

Dyer, L., and T. Reeves. (1995). "Human Resource Strategies and Firm Performance: What Do We Know and Where Do We Need to Go?" *International Journal of Human Resource Management* 6: 656-70.

Edmans, A. (2011). "Does the Stock Market Fully Value Intangibles? Employee Satisfaction and Equity Prices." *Journal of Financial Economics* 101: 621-40.

Ekeh, Peter P. (1974). *Social Exchange Theory: The Two Traditions*. Cambridge, MA: Harvard University Press.

Faldetta, G. (2011). "The Logic of Gift and Gratuitousness in Business Relationships." *Journal of Business Ethics* 100 (Suppl.): S67-77.

Faleye, O., and E. Trahan. (2011). "Labor-Friendly Corporate Practices: Is What Is Good for Employees Good for Shareholders?" *Journal of Business Ethics* 101: 1-27.

Falk, A. (2007). "Gift Exchange in the Field." *Econometrica* 75, no. 5: 1501-11.

Ferrary, M. (2003). "The Gift Exchange in the Social Networks of Silicon Valley." *California Management Review* 45, no. 4: 120-38.

Fisher, R. J. (2007). "Business Marketing and the Ethics of Gift Giving." *Industrial Marketing Management* 36: 99-108.

Fulmer, I. S., B. Gerhart, and K. Scott. (2003). "Are the 100 Best Better? An Empirical Investigation of the Relationship between Being a 'Great Place to Work' and Firm Performance." *Personnel Psychology* 56: 965-93.

Giesler, Markus. (September 2006). "Consumer Gift System: Netnographic Insights from Napster." *Journal of Consumer Research* 33: 283-90.

Gouldner, Alvin. (April 1960). "The Norm of Reciprocity."
American Sociological Review 25: 161–78.

Granovetter, Mark. (November 1985). "Economic Action and Social
Structure: The Problem of Embeddedness." *American Journal of
Sociology* 91: 481–510.

Gratton, L., & Erickson, T. J. (2007, November). Eight ways to build
collaborative teams. Harvard Business Review, 85(11), 100-110.

Haas, David F., and Forrest A. Deseran. (March 1981). "Trust and
Symbolic Exchange." *Social Psychology Quarterly* 44: 3–13.

Hemenway, David. (1984). *Prices and Choices: Microeconomic
Vignettes*. Cambridge, MA: Ballinger.

Homans, George C. (1961). *Social Behavior: Its Elementary Forms*.
New York: Harcourt, Brace & World.

Kahneman, Daniel, and Amos Tversky. (1979). "Prospect Theory:
An Analysis of Decision Under Risk." *Econometrica* 47, no. 2: 263–92.

Kehoe, Rebecca R., and Patrick M. Wright. (2013). "The Impact
of High-Performance Human Resource Practices on Employees'
Attitudes and Behaviors." *Journal of Management* 39, no. 2: 366–91.

Kelly, J. E. (2004). "Solidarity and Subsidiarity: 'Organizing principles' for Corporate Moral Leadership in the New Global Economy." *Journal of Business Ethics* 52, no. 3: 283–95.

Komter, Aafke. (2005). *Social Solidarity and the Gift*. Cambridge: Cambridge University Press.

Levi-Strauss, C. (1965). "The Principle of Reciprocity." In *Sociological Theory*. Edited by L. A. Coser and B. Rosenberg. New York: Macmillan.

Lowrey, T.A., C. C. Otnes, and J. A. Ruth. (2004). "Social Influences on Dyadic Giving Over Time: A Taxonomy from the Giver's Perspective." *Journal of Consumer Research* 30: 547–58.

Luo, Y. (2003). "Industrial Dynamics and Managerial Networking in an Emerging Market: The Case of China." *Strategic Management Journal* 24: 1315–27

Maheswaran, D., and J. Meyers-Levy. (1990). "The Influence of Message Framing and Issue Involvement." *Journal of Marketing Research* 27: 361–67.

Mauss, Marcel. (1925). *The Gift: Form and Functions of Exchange in Archaic Societies*. New York: Norton.

Mauss, Marcel. (1954). *The Gift: Form and Functions of Exchange in Archaic Societies.* Translated by Ian Cunnison. London: Cohen & West.

Mauss, M. and D. W. Halls. (2000). *Gift: The Form and Reason for Exchange in Archaic Societies.* New York: Norton.

Mills, Judson, and Margaret S. Clark. (1982). "Exchange and Communal Relationships." *Review of Personality and Social Psychology* 3. Later published in book form. Edited by Ladd Wheeler. Beverly Hills, CA: Sage. 1–144.

Molm, L.D., N. Takahashi, and G> Peterson. (2000). "Risk and Trust in Social Exchange: An Experimental Test of a Classical Proposition." *American Journal of Sociology* 105: 1396–1428.

Nishii, L. H., and P. M. Wright. (2008). "Variability within Organizations: Implications for Strategic Human Resources Management." In *The People Make the Place: Dynamic Linkages between Individuals and Organizations.* Edited by. Mahwah, NJ: Erlbaum. 225–

Posner, Richard A. (1980). "A Theory of Primitive Society, with Special References to Law." *Journal of Law and Economics* 23: 1–53.

Provis, C. (2008). "Guanxi and Conflicts of Interest." *Journal of Business Ethics* 79(1/2): 57–68.

Renneboog, L., J. Ter Horst, and C. Zhang. (2008b). "The Price of Ethics and Stakeholder Governance: The Performance of Socially Responsible Mutual Funds." *Journal of Corporate Finance* 14: 302–28.

Rothschild, Michael, and Joseph Stiglitz. (1976). "Equilibrium in Competitive Insurance Markets: An Essay in the Economics of Imperfect Information." *Quarterly Journal of Economics* 90: 629–49.

Rousseau, D. (1990). "New Hire Perceptions of Their Own and Their Employer's Obligations: A Study of Psychological Contracts." *Journal of Organizational Behavior* 5: 389–400.

Ruth, Julie A., Cele C. Otnes, and Frederic F. Brunel. (1999). "Gift Receipt and the Reformulation of Interpersonal Relationships." *Journal of Consumer Research* 25: 385–402.

Schrift, A. D., ed. (1997). *The Logic of the Gift: Toward an Ethic of Generosity*. New York: Routledge.

Schultz, P. W., J. M. Nolan, R. B. Cialdini, N. J. Goldstein, and V. Griskevicius. (2007). "The Constructive, Destructive, and Reconstructive Power of Social Norms." *Psychological Science* 18: 429–34.

Shaw, Brian. (April 26, 2014). "Glassdoor Ratings Might Predict Stock Market Outperformance." Motley Fool Blog. Available at http://www.fool.com/investing/general/2014/04/26/great-leaders-drive-great-stock-performance.aspx.

Sherry, J. F., Jr. (1983). "Gift Giving in Anthropological Perspective."
Journal of Consumer Research: 157–68.

Snider, J., R. P. Hill, and D. Martin. (2003). "Corporate Social
Responsibility in the 21st Century: A View from the World's Most
Successful Firms." *Journal of Business Ethics* 48, no. 2: 175–87.

Snow, D. A., and R. D. Benford. (1992). "Master Frames and Cycles
of Protest." *In Frontiers in Social Movement Theory*. Edited by
Aldon D. Morris and Carol McClurg Mueller. New Haven, CT: Yale
University Press. 133–55.

Standifird, S., and R. Marshall. (2000). "The Transaction Cost
Advantage of Guanxi-Based Business Practices." *Journal of World
Business* 35: 21–43.

Thaler, Richard H. (1987). "The Psychology and Economics
Conference Handbook: Comments on Simon, on Einhorn and
Hogarth, and on Tversky and Kahneman." In *Rational Choice:
The Contrast Between Economics and Psychology*. Edited by R. M.
Hogarth and M. W. Reder. Chicago: University of Chicago Press.

Trivers, R. (1985). *Social Evolution*. Menlo Park, CA: Benjamin/
Cummings.

Tsui, A. S., D. X. Wang, and Y. C. Zhang. (2002). "Employment Relationship with Chinese Middle Managers: Exploring Differences between State-Owned and Non-State-Owned Firms." In *The Management of Enterprises in the People's Republic of China*. Edited by A. S. Tsui, and C. M. Lau. Dordrecht: Kluwer. 347-74.

Tversky, A., and D. Kahneman. (1981). "The Framing of Decisions and the Psychology of Choice." *Science* 211: 453-58.

Verhezen, P. (2009). *Gifts, Corruption, Philanthropy: The Ambiguity of Gift Practices in Business*. Oxford: Peter Lang.

Wilson, Timothy, D. Centerbar, D. Kermer, and Daniel Gilbert. (2005). "The Pleasures of Uncertainty: Prolonging Positive Moods in Ways People Do Not Anticipate." *Journal of Personality and Social Psychology* 88, no. 1: 5-21.

Wright, P., W. F. Szeto, and L. T. W. Cheng. (2002). "Guanxi and Professional Conduct in China: A Management Development Perspective." *International Journal of Human Resource Management* 13: 156-82.

Zelizer, Vivian A. (September 1989). "The Social Meanings of Money: 'Special Monies.'" *American Journal of Sociology* 95: 342-77.

ABOUT THE AUTHOR

———

JOHN RUHLIN is the founder of The Ruhlin Group, a gift logistics company that helps clients like the Chicago Cubs, Wells Fargo, Caesar's Entertainment, Miami Dolphins, Morgan Stanley, and The John Maxwell Company execute year-round gifting strategies.

John's unique approach to relationships led him to become the #1 salesman for a $250 Million direct sales company by the time he was 23 (out of 1.5 Million reps). He now speaks widely about strategic gifting and relationship building and helps CEOs and sales teams drive referrals and open doors to elusive decision makers.